FLOWERS

The Secrets of a Colorful Garden

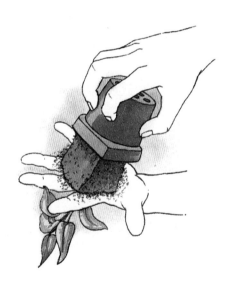

Publications International, Ltd.

Barbara W. Ellis is a freelance writer, editor, and lifelong gardener. She has authored numerous gardening books, including *Covering Ground* (2007) and *The Veggie Gardener's Answer Book* (2008). Barbara lives in Maryland on the Eastern Shore of the Chesapeake Bay.

CONTENTS

Creating Seasons of Color

If you've always dreamed of having a beautiful flower garden filled with colorful, thriving plants, but you didn't know quite where to start, get ready. This book makes that dream possible. In it you'll find out how expert gardeners keep their beds and borders overflowing with flowers week after week. You'll discover how to combine colors like a pro. And you'll learn the secrets to selecting healthy annuals and perennials at the garden center (and making your money go further), starting your own flowers from seed, and caring for your flowers with a minimum of fuss.

PLANNING A BEAUTIFUL FLOWER GARDEN

The best place to start the design process is by deciding what kind of garden you want, and where you should plant it. Would you like a small flower bed in the backyard or by the front door? Or are you picturing a larger garden surrounding your terrace that includes patio containers or several flower beds? Starting small is certainly best. You can always enlarge a garden later, but keeping its size manageable helps minimize the amount of work required to create and care for it.

Nestled along a quiet backyard path, this garden is guaranteed to be visited and enjoyed frequently.

Know Your Site

The best garden plans are grounded in reality. Take time to analyze your growing conditions before you create a design or buy plants. No plant looks good if it is suffering. Although you can sometimes alter growing conditions, the best approach is to know what conditions your site offers and then to look for plants that will thrive in those conditions. (See pages 19–22 for information on assessing and improving soil.)

For a successful garden, stick to perennials and annuals that will thrive in the amount of sun or shade your site receives.

Sun and Shade

Watch how sunlight and shadows play over your yard to determine how much light a site receives before you create a design or select plants for that site. Gardeners and garden centers use the following terms to describe amounts of sun and shade:

Full sun. This is the easiest exposure to describe: Sites that receive six to eight hours of direct sun a day are in full sun.

Light shade. Sites that are shaded for part of the day but in direct sun for a good portion of it are located in light shade. You'll find light-shade sites under mature trees, because the sun can shine directly onto the ground beneath their high leaf canopy.

Partial shade. Filtered light, or partial shade, can be found under trees that allow sunlight to penetrate through the canopy and dapple the ground throughout the day.

East or West?

Sites on the east side and sites on the west side of shade-casting trees or buildings may receive equal hours of sun and shade, but they don't produce identical results. Gardens on east-facing sites receive cool morning sun and afternoon shade. Use them for plants that may burn in hot sun. West-facing gardens, shaded in the morning and exposed to hot sun in the afternoon, are better for sun-loving plants.

Deep shade. Full, or deep, shade is the most difficult lighting condition. It is found under thickly branched trees or evergreens. A garden located in deep shade receives little or no direct sun. You might, however, be able to remove some lower branches from trees, thin out overcrowded branches in the canopy, or remove smaller scraggly or unwanted saplings and brush to brighten a densely shaded spot.

Settling on a Garden Shape

To help you settle on a shape and size, consider the three traditional types of gardens:

Flower beds. These are typically located close to a house or patio and can be viewed from all sides. They can be any size and located in sun or shade. (Plan on installing pathways through large beds so you can get in to tend and enjoy the plants.) Flower beds can feature all kinds of flowers of varying shapes and textures and contain an interesting mix of foliage and blooms.

Plants in a flower bed are generally low to the ground, so you can see the entire bed at once.

Borders. These are large gardens that typically run along a fence or building. In a small- or medium-size yard, the total length of the border(s) should be no more than half the width of the yard. For example, a 40-foot-wide yard could have a single 20-foot border or two 10-foot-long ones. Borders are generally 5 to 8 feet deep, with a narrow path in back so you can reach the center of the border from the front or back to tend plants.

Island beds. Often oval or kidney shape, these are surrounded by lawn and can be viewed from all sides. An island bed needs to be wide enough to look substantial from your front porch, patio, or kitchen window—wherever you will typically be when you see it.

A good rule of thumb: The width of an island bed should equal half the distance from where you view it. For example, if an island bed is 20 feet away, it should be 10 feet wide. (You may need to create a path through the island bed to tend the plants.)

DECIDING WHAT TO GROW

While you can grow a garden that features only annuals or only perennials, there's no rule that says your garden can't include both—and more. In fact, the most appealing gardens are often creative blends of annuals and perennials, some with a sprinkling of roses, herbs, flowering shrubs, trees, bulbs, and even ornamental vegetables, as well.

A mixed garden makes especially good sense these days, when we all have too much to do and not enough time to do it. A mixed garden allows you to add plants as needed—whether annuals, perennials, herbs, or bulbs. You can plant extra annuals to fill unexpected empty spots, for example. Or you can include a new flower that was a gift from a friend or was just introduced at your garden center. A mixed garden also allows you to feature personal favorites and create a landscape that truly reflects your own individual taste.

Flower Types

Walk around a garden center or turn the pages of a seed catalog, and you'll see terms like annuals, perennials, and bulbs. But what do these terms mean, and how do you use them when planning a garden?

Annuals. These germinate, bloom, set seed, and die all in one season. You'll often see these plants described as either cool- or warm-weather

Drifts of bold-colored salvia, petunias, celosia, and dusty miller combine to make a dramatic garden of annuals.

annuals. *Cool-weather annuals,* including pansies and alyssum, grow best in spring and fall, when temperatures are cool. They also can be grown through winter in the south. *Warm-weather annuals,* including marigolds and zinnias, thrive in hot summer weather. Knowing whether a plant is a warm- or cool-season annual is essential to scheduling it for top performance in your garden.

Another group of plants that are commonly treated as annuals are plants that are killed by frost at the end of the season. They include begonias and coleus. Also called *tender perennials,* these can be dug out in fall and overwintered indoors in areas of the country where they are not hardy—in other words, where they will not survive the typical winter weather. You can also take and root cuttings of many tender perennials.

Perennials. Living two or more seasons, perennials need to be hardy, or able to survive winter cold, in a region. Peonies and daylilies are both long-lived perennials. Columbines are short-lived perennials that need to be replaced every couple years. See the Hardiness Zone Map on page 80 to determine the average minimum winter low temperatures in your region, then use that information and the hardiness information from seed packets, plant tags, and/or seed catalogs to select perennials suitable for your garden.

Biennials. These plants produce foliage the first year and flowers the second. Foxglove and hollyhock are both biennials. Like most biennials, they *self-sow,* producing new plants and flowers in subsequent years without any human help. You can sometimes grow biennials as annuals if you start them early, causing them to bloom the first season. Many will live a few years as short-lived perennials.

Herbs for Flower Gardens

Mix fragrant, attractive herbs such as these with your annuals and perennials to make your garden beautiful *and* useful.

Basil	Dill	Rosemary
Chamomile	Lavender	Sage
Chives	Parsley	Thyme

Bulbs. These are plants with fleshy underground structures. They include true bulbs, such as daffodils, and plants with fleshy roots and stems, such as dahlias and tuberous begonias.

Herbs. This term is used to refer to any plant valued for its flavor, fragrance, or medicinal properties. Examples include basil, lavender, and rosemary.

Selecting Annuals and Perennials

Whether you are plotting out a design on paper or pushing a shopping cart through a garden center, it's hard to know which annuals and perennials to pick. There are just so many beautiful choices! The following tips can help you select the best plants for your garden:

- Choose annuals and perennials that will thrive in the amount of sun or shade your garden receives. No amount of wishing will make sun-loving plants thrive in shade, or shade plants in sun.

- For season-long color in a dull spot, use groups of annuals. If you want to dress up an all-green shrub border, for example, try adding a few groupings of annuals in front of the shrubs to inject an extra burst of color.

- Use annuals to give a perennial garden a much-needed midsummer boost. Add summer-blooming annuals in the spaces where spring bulbs, pansies, or early blooming perennials are dying back. You can pop them into any empty spots that appear.

> ### Plants for Shade
> You'll find more options once you start shopping, but this list will get you started.
>
> **Perennials**
> Hostas, ferns, hellebores, astilbes, epimediums, daylilies, hardy geraniums
>
> **Annuals**
> Browallia, impatiens, begonias, coleus, alyssum, torenia, violas
>
> **Bulbs**
> Caladiums, tuberous begonias. Daffodils and other early blooming spring bulbs are also great for adding color to a shade garden at the start of the growing season.

- Pay special attention to foliage. This is especially important when selecting perennials, since they typically are only in bloom for a few weeks each year. Attractive foliage is the foundation of a well-designed garden.
- Ask for recommendations. Gardening neighbors and friends, along with nursery or garden-center personnel, will be happy to help you select plants that will thrive in your area.

PLAYING WITH COLOR

Just as you'd think about color before painting a room, it's a good idea to consider flower color when you select annuals, perennials, and other plants for your garden. Do you enjoy bold colors like reds and oranges or pastels like pink and pale blue? One way to select colors to use in your garden is to consider color temperature.

Drifts of solid-color perennials or annuals, such as these bearded irises and lavender, make an eye-catching color statement.

Warm colors. These are bold and appear visually to be closer to you than they actuallly are. Warm colors are the colors of fire—red, orange, and brilliant yellow. They add warmth and excitement to a garden and are especially suitable for a garden located farther away from your house.

Cool colors. Cool colors—the colors of water—recede from the eye and appear to be farther away than they really are. Blues, purples, silvers, and whites are calming and cooling and can be very soothing during the heat of summer. Cool-colored flowers

Yellow and orange marigolds and hot-colored red salvias, set off by dusty miller, add warmth and excitement to this garden.

create pleasant, quiet gardens close to the house, but they may get lost if placed farther away.

Using Color in the Garden

For best results, it's a good idea to limit your color choices to a few that form a pleasing color scheme. Here are some ideas to get you started:

Consider backdrops. Existing backgrounds, including fences, house walls, flowering shrubs, and other major landscape features will affect your choice of flower colors. For example, if your house is painted white, you probably won't want to plant white flowers against it, because they'll be virtually invisible. If your garden is backed by dark woods or evergreens, flowers in dark shades of blue and purple will disappear against them, while white, yellow, silver-gray, and yellow-green blooms will stand out.

Use color to set the mood. Think about the mood and atmosphere you'd like to create in each area of your garden. Create a nostalgic, romantic look by using pale pastels, or display a modern, upbeat style by mixing pure bright colors.

Using complementary colors, located across from one another on the color wheel, adds excitement to a garden. Mix purple flowers with yellow ones, for example, or blues with oranges. For a restful scheme, pick analogous colors—colors like blue and purple that are adjacent on the wheel. Varying the intensity of different flower colors in your design will often help add vitality and interest, as well.

Give white and silver a try. White flowers heighten the contrast of any other colors you select. You can also use silver flowers or foliage to separate contrasting colors in a design.

Don't worry—experiment. Although you'll want to plan the colors for your garden with care, inevitably some of your choices will not work out as happily as you'd envisioned. Don't be too worried about getting it all exactly right in advance. You can always move or remove those plants that do not blend well.

Massing

The easiest, most straightforward way to use color in a garden is to select one favorite hue and flood the entire planting area with it. With this approach, you won't need to decide which colors and textures blend well together. If you streamline your approach even further and go with a single type of plant in a single color, you'll also eliminate the need to decide where a particular variety should be placed. Plus, you won't need to learn the cultural requirements of more than one kind of plant. This single-plant solution can be a money-saver, too: If you're growing annuals, you only need to buy one or two packets of seed to obtain enough plants to fill an entire planting area. Such massed plantings are generally rather formal looking—bold and dramatic rather than homey or quaint—so they're the perfect complement to a large or formal house. Massing can also provide a clean, uncluttered look for very small gardens.

Look Indoors for Ideas

If you can't decide what colors to pick and simply don't know where to start, look to a favorite pillow, painting, rug, or fabric for a color scheme, then select plants with flowers in similar colors.

Drifts

There are more sophisticated ways to use color, though. The best approach is to arrange the annuals and perennials in groups of three to several plants called drifts. Arranging plants in drifts ensures that the garden doesn't end up looking like a sloppy scramble of unrelated hues, all screaming for attention. When flowers are arranged in drifts, individual colors have added impact and visual weight.

Repetition

A well-designed garden presents a unified picture, and you can use color to create that unity. Select a favorite color, then repeat it throughout the garden. You can use one plant variety to do this—interspersing groups of yellow marigolds, for example. Or, you can use drifts of different but like-colored varieties—lemon-yellow daylilies, coreopsis, and marigolds, for example—throughout the garden. Mix them with drifts of annuals and perennials in other colors, and you'll create a pleasing, unified design.

Repeating colors, in this case purples and pinks, helps turn separate plantings in a garden into a unified whole.

Planning for Constant Bloom

While most annuals bloom all summer long, the majority of perennials have a limited season of bloom. So unless you opt for a garden built solely of annuals, you'll need to do a little planning to ensure that you will have new flowers coming into bloom week after week. That planning will pay ongoing dividends, though, as you relish the anticipation and excitement of watching new flowers burst into bloom throughout the growing season. Use the following tips to guide your planning:

Build up your perennial repertoire. Perennials are the backbone of any garden, providing reliable beauty with minimal maintenance, and you'll want to have some blooming throughout your growing season. If you find yourself short of perennials that flower during certain times, check the lists on pages 14–15 for ideas. You can also ask other gardeners and garden-center personnel in your area for perennial suggestions.

Bank on bulbs. Daffodils and other spring bulbs are great for adding spring color to the garden. And summer-blooming bulbs such as lilies, gladiolus, cannas, dahlias, and tuberous begonias add visual punch to early summer gardens.

Bridge gaps with annuals. Of course, combining annuals with your perennials is one way to ensure that you will have something pretty to look at all season long. But annuals can be especially useful in perking up your garden from midsummer to early fall, when summertime heat and humidity reduce the number of perennials that are in bloom.

To identify the plants that will add the most to your garden, start by listing all the flowers you know you want to include.

Perennials for Every Season

The following lists can help you select perennials for each part of the growing season.

EARLY SPRING

Hellebore (*Helleborus* species)
Epimedium (*Epimedium* species)
Lungwort (*Pulmonaria* species)

Spring

LATE SPRING/EARLY SUMMER

Bleeding heart (*Dicentra* species)
Candytuft (*Iberis sempervirens*)
Columbine (*Aquilegia* species)
False, or wild, indigo (*Baptisia australis*)
Foxglove (*Digitalis purpurea*)
Iris (*Iris* species)
Peony (*Paeonia* species)
Pink (*Dianthus* species)
Poppy, Oriental (*Papaver orientale*)

EARLY TO MIDDLE SUMMER

Plants marked with a + bloom until late summer or early fall.
Achillea, yarrow (*Achillea* species)
Astilbe (*Astilbe* species)
Beardtongue (*Penstemon barbatus*)
Blanketflower (*Gaillardia* × *grandiflora*)+
Butterfly weed (*Asclepias tuberosa*)+
Cardinal flower (*Lobelia cardinalis*)

Early Summer

Indicate bloom times after each name. Then look down your list and make sure you have some plants listed for each season.

BEYOND FLOWERS

It's easy to get swept away by flowers, but you won't regret looking beyond blooms when selecting plants for your garden.

Coreopsis (*Coreopsis* species)+
Daylily (*Hemerocallis* species)+
Monarda, bee balm (*Monarda didyma*)
Rudbeckia, orange coneflower (*Rudbeckia* species)+
Painted daisy (*Tanacetum coccineum*)
Shasta daisy (*Leucanthemum × superbum*)
Stokesia, Stoke's aster (*Stokesia laevis*)
Verbascum (*Verbascum* species)+

Late Summer

MIDDLE TO LATE SUMMER
Aster (*Aster* species)
Goldenrod (*Solidago* species)
Hibiscus, rose mallow (*Hibiscus moscheutos*)
Lavender (*Lavandula angustifolia*)
Purple coneflower (*Echinacea purpurea*)
Garden phlox (*Phlox paniculata*)
Scabiosa, pincushion flower (*Scabiosa caucasica*)
Salvia (*Salvia* species)

LATE SUMMER/FALL
Aster (*Aster* species)
Chrysanthemum (*Leucanthemum* species)
Eupatorium (*Eupatorium* species)
Japanese anemone (*Anemone* species)
Perovskia, Russian sage (*Perovskia* species)
Toad lily (*Tricyrtis* species)

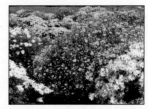
Fall

Consider Foliage

Perennials and annuals with outstanding foliage—leaves that look good all season or are colorfully patterned—are invaluable in the garden. Hostas are well known for bold leaves in shades from deep green to chartreuse, many with lighter markings. Silver-leaved dusty miller and colorful coleus are annuals grown for their foliage.

Try to include plants that sport leaves of different shapes and sizes and foliage of varying textures (shiny, matt, rough, smooth, etc.), as well. Incorporating plants with assorted leaf styles adds contrast and interest to a garden, making it more dramatic and appealing. Achilleas and astilbes have feathery leaves, for example, while daylilies and ornamental grasses sport ribbonlike leaves. Attractive leaves also set off flowers more effectively.

Hostas, shown here with ferns, are among the finest perennials for colorful foliage. Use them in partial to full shade.

On your plant list, put a star next to any that have attractive leaves. If you need additional plants with eye-catching foliage, check the final chapter of this book, Easy Garden Flowers.

Mix Heights and Forms

Pay attention to height, too, as you select plants for your garden. Include plants of differing height, so you have short selections for the front edges and taller ones to use in the middle of beds or at the back of borders.

Another variable to consider is shape, or form—in terms of both the plant as a whole and its flowers. Peonies and Shasta daisies, for example, have rounded forms. To make your garden more visually interesting, consider mixing such rounded plants with vase-shape plants such as daylilies and vertical plants like hollyhock and foxglove.

CREATING A DESIGN

The idea of selecting and arranging plants and colors in a garden probably sounds overwhelming, but don't get discouraged. Start by reviewing your plant list. For a small- to medium-size garden, you'll need six to eight perennials, plus some annuals and bulbs. There are two basic ways you can approach turning your list into a garden. One way involves planning the garden on paper; the other consists of shopping for the plants on your list and arranging them on the site. Either way, you'll

This garden uses a variety of forms and heights to create a colorful, appealing sitting area.

avoid a common mistake most new gardeners make, because you'll already have a plant list before you purchase a single flower.

Before you start, review your list and confirm that each plant will thrive on your chosen site. Eliminate any plants that won't grow well there, and substitute more suitable ones.

Putting a Garden on Paper

Planning a flower garden can be a fairly complex undertaking. Ideally, you are trying to keep track of a host of details—light and soil preferences, plant height and size, blooming schedule, bloom color and form, foliage characteristics, and plant growth habits. The best place to start is with a simple sketch. Draw a quick outline of your garden bed, noting its approximate dimensions and the amount of sun the area receives each day. Divide it into blocks or rounded blobs to denote drifts of different plants.

Next, begin filling in plant names. Think about what each flower looks like as you decide where to add it on your paper plan. If you are planning a border, put the tallest plants in the back, with shorter ones in front. For flower beds, put the tallest plants in the center. If possible, use colored pencils so you can write each plant's name or shade its designated space in the color of its flower. This will help you spread out the colors, so you don't end up with all the reds at one end. In addition, if you have the information available, estimate how many of each plant you'll need by looking at the recommended spacing for each one and comparing it to the amount of space in your plan.

As you work, avoid clumping all the plants that bloom at the same time in one part of the garden. Yes, grouping plants that bloom together can create greater visual impact. But you also want color throughout the bed. Try instead to create a rhythm by interspersing small clusters of plants that flower together throughout the border or bed. Next to an early-flowering group, place a mid-season and a late-season group, and then repeat. Be sure to have a balance of early, mid-season, and late bloomers mixed throughout the planting area.

Finally, see whether or not your design is well balanced. Check to be certain no tall plants are in front of shorter ones unless the tall ones are thin and airy. Be sure there are no adjoining colors that are likely to clash. And confirm that no shade lovers have been placed in a sunny bed, or vice versa. Inevitably, you will need to make changes and substitutions as your garden grows, but by carefully studying your plan in advance, you can correct obvious mistakes ahead of time.

Planning on the Ground

The other planning option is to take your plant list to the garden center and buy your plants. Then, set out the pots on your prepared site in the arrangement you think will look best. Stand back and study it, adjust the grouping, and repeat until you are happy with the arrangement. Check plant labels to confirm the spacing requirements of perennials, and make sure everything has the room it needs. Perennials will look sparse the first year or two at their recommended spacing. Until they mature, plan on seating annuals between them to give the garden a full, lush look. Once you have an arrangement you like, start planting.

Installing Your Garden Successfully

Getting your garden off to a good start is an important and enjoyable process with a big payoff. The time and care you put in at this stage—from incorporating soil amendments, sowing seed or buying plants, fussing over transplants, shifting annuals and perennials until the arrangement is just right, and finally tucking your plants into their garden bed—are well worth the effort. Your reward will be a gorgeous display of flowers.

UNDERSTANDING YOUR SOIL

Good soil is essential to a great garden. The loose, dark earth from which fabulous gardens spring doesn't usually just happen. It is created by gardeners. Whether you have dry, sandy soil that water runs straight through or heavy clay that stays wet for days before drying to the hardness of concrete, there's one thing you can do to improve it: Add organic matter. Digging plentiful doses of organic material—chopped leaves, ground-up twigs, rotted livestock manure, old lawn clippings—into the earth will improve and nourish any kind of soil, making it ideal for growing plants. *Compost,*

Organic matter is the secret to improving any garden soil.

made from decayed leaves, grass clippings, other yard waste, and even food scraps, is the single best choice for boosting soil. You can make your own, purchase it bagged at a garden center, or perhaps even get it free or at little cost from your city or town.

Identify Your Soil Type

There are various ways to determine which kind of soil you're dealing with. For a quick test, simply squeeze some slightly moist soil in your hand. *Clay soil* forms a dense, compact lump that retains its shape. *Sandy soil* doesn't hold its shape at all. And *loam soil* forms a ball that falls apart if tapped with a finger. While adding compost and other organic matter will help all of these soil types, the following specific guidelines will help you fine-tune your garden's foundation:

Clay soil. Never dig or plant in clay soil when it is wet. Be especially careful to avoid walking on clay soil, as well; it has a very dense structure, and walking on it compresses the small pores that hold the air and water that a plant's roots need.

If your soil is pure clay or drains poorly despite amendments, consider using a raised bed: With landscape ties or stone, construct a frame at least 6 inches tall, then fill the bed with high-quality topsoil purchased from a garden center. Mix in organic matter, mulch the soil, and give it a few weeks to settle before planting.

Sandy soil. Keep sandy soil mulched at all times to hold it in place and help retain moisture. And get in the habit of adding compost every time you dig, since microbes in the soil use up organic matter quickly.

Loam soil. This is the ideal garden soil, but don't rest on your laurels if you have it! Add compost and other organic matter regularly, and keep the soil mulched to protect it.

Consider Additional Testing

More sophisticated testing—such as a complete soil test—can provide you with even more valuable information. Your local cooperative extension service may be able to handle this for you.

If not, you'll need to send a sample of your soil to a private laboratory. First, contact the service or lab for directions on how you should gather your soil sample, then follow them closely. When you send in your sample, indicate whether you prefer recommendations for organic or chemical soil amendments. The test results you receive in return will indicate your soil's pH level—how acidic or alkaline it is—and its nutrient needs and will recommend ways to improve it. Add only the nutrients and amendments your soil report says are necessary. Using more is not better and may be counterproductive.

PREPARING THE GARDEN BED

Before planting that first flower in your new garden bed, you must first deal with any grass or weeds on the site. Traditionally, gardeners have pulled up sod, dug out weeds, and turned the site by hand or with a rototiller—and certainly this is the quicker method. But if you have time, you can just heavily mulch the site and wait for the grass and weeds to die instead. Either way, begin by marking the flower bed's boundaries: Use stakes and string to mark a square or rectangular bed and a garden hose to outline a bed with curved edges.

The Traditional Method

First, dig up any weeds. Then remove any grass by cutting through the sod to create roughly two-foot-wide strips, slicing off the roots by sliding a spade under the grass, and pulling or rolling up each strip like a rug. Remove the sod from the entire bed; you can turn it upside down on your compost pile or use pieces to patch dead spots elsewhere in your lawn.

Once the grass and leaves are gone, dig up the area, removing rocks as you go. Next, spread two to four inches of well-rotted manure, compost, or leaf mold over the site to improve soil quality. Then hand-turn (using a spade or garden fork) or rototill the bed to a depth of six to eight inches to really work the organic matter into the soil. Rake the bed smooth, and cover it with mulch. Leave the bed unplanted for at least two weeks, so the soil has time to settle before planting. Every three to four days, stir the top inch or two of soil with a hoe or cultivator to eradicate fast-germinating weeds; this will make your weeding chores lighter during the rest of the season.

The Smothering Approach

Another very effective option for preparing a garden bed—one that avoids digging altogether—involves smothering existing grass and weeds. Start by mowing or cutting the grass and weeds as close to the soil as possible. Next, cover the site with a layer of newspapers eight to ten sheets thick. (If it's windy, spread a section, then quickly wet it or top it with a shovel of compost or mulch to keep it from blowing away.) Top the papers with a one- to two-inch-thick layer of compost, clean topsoil, mulch, or chopped leaves. Wait at least three months before planting. At planting time, just dig straight through the layers.

Smothering is a great method to use if you have time to prepare beds in fall for spring planting or in spring for fall planting. Since it eliminates heavy digging, it's also a great option for gardeners with back problems or other health issues.

Install edging strips around the bed to keep grass from invading the flower bed and keep flowers from spreading into the lawn; it'll save many hours of maintenance each year. Buy and install plastic edging, or make a brick or stone barrier at least two inches deep and six inches wide. The top of the edging should be at ground level so you can run one wheel of the lawnmower just inside the bed and trim as you mow.

STARTING FROM SEED

While buying flats of annuals and pots of perennials is tempting because they create an instant display in the garden, starting your own flowers from seed makes sense for a variety of reasons. Many annuals and perennials, for example, are not commercially available as established plants, often because they simply don't transplant successfully and must be grown from seed. Starting from seed also makes sense if you have a large garden and need lots

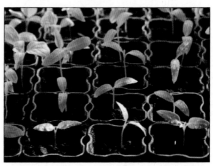

You can start seed indoors in market packs or individual pots, such as those shown here, or you can sow seed directly into the garden bed.

of plants to fill it. You can grow dozens of plants from seed for the cost of a single established perennial.

How to Start Seed Indoors

You can start seed indoors by sowing them in a pot of soil on a windowsill, but you'll get better results if you make a small initial investment in seed-starting equipment and supplies.

For best results indoors, consider investing in a seed-starting setup with lights.

Preparing Your Indoor Nursery

To give your seeds the best start in life, you'll need to provide the following elements in your indoor nursery:

Light. The most essential ingredient for successful seed starting is adequate light. Seedlings that do not receive enough light will stretch out toward the light source and become leggy. Invest in special grow lamps, or buy a simple fluorescent shop light and hang it with chain and "S" hooks so you can adjust the distance between it and the seedlings. (Maintain about three inches between the light and the plant tops at all times.) Add a timer to turn lights on and off automatically. Give plants 16 to 18 hours of light daily. Don't leave the lights on constantly; darkness is also essential.

Heat. Bottom heat is another secret to successful seed starting. You can set trays of seedlings on a radiator or atop the refrigerator, but for best results, buy a commercial heat mat designed to heat soil.

Soil. Although you can mix your own potting soil, it is simpler to pur-chase specially formulated seed-starting mix. Before filling potting containers, dump the mix in a large bucket or tub, add plenty of warm water, and

Specially designed mats that provide heat from beneath the soil speed germination. They are also ideal for rooting cuttings.

stir. Wait until the mix has soaked up the water before filling the containers with it.

Containers. Seeds can be started in a variety of containers, provided the containers hold soil and allow easy passage of water through drainage holes. You can use milk cartons or plastic food containers with holes punched in the bottom, or you can pur-chase plastic pots or six-pack trays, fiber pots or trays, or special seed-starting kits. Containers designed to hold a single plant (three-inch pots are a good size) are best for large plants, which tend to crowd each other out in six-packs. You will also need flats (shallow trays) to catch water dripping from pots.

Planting Seeds

Once the containers are filled with moistened starting mix, check the seed packets for sowing directions. Sow two to three seeds in each pot, or broadcast seed over the surface of larger containers. If the seeds are very small, don't cover them with additional soil; just press them into the mix. After broadcasting medium to large seeds, however,

sprinkle starting mix over them, then lightly press the surface of the mix. Label each pot/tray with the plant name and date sown.

After sowing the seeds, water the pots or trays from the bottom: Set the pots or trays in a flat with about one inch of warm water in the bottom, and let them soak up the water until the mix feels moist. Allow excess water to drip out the bottom of each pot or tray before placing it in your growing setup. Cover the containers loosely with plastic to maintain high humidity. Check them daily for signs of germination (sprouting).

As soon as seedlings sprout, begin feeding with a soluble fertilizer at one-quarter the dilution recommended for mature plants. Check daily to make sure the planting mix is moist enough, and if the soil feels more dry than wet, water them from the bottom for five or ten minutes.

When the seedlings produce their second set of true leaves, thin them by cutting off this second set with sharp scissors to give the seedlings space to grow properly.

Moving Seedlings into Pots

Seedlings in large containers or trays need to be transplanted to individual pots when the first true leaves appear. To do this,

Always handle seedlings carefully: Hold them by a leaf, never by the stem, which is easily damaged. Place the seedling in the new container so the soil line will be at the same level on the stem as it was in the seed tray. Gently firm the soil around the roots. Water from the top with a weak fertilizer solution. Then place the plants back by the window or under grow lamps to continue growing.

gently lift them out, separate them carefully, and replant them in individual pots following the directions in the above caption.

Seeding Perennials: A Special Case

Compared to annuals, many perennials take longer to germinate from seed. They may also require special handling. For example, they may need to be exposed to several months of cool temperatures in order to germinate. A simple way to deal with these requirements is to sow seeds in pots, mulch them with fine gravel (like that used in aquariums), and set them outside in a protected location to germinate. Sow pots in winter for spring germination.

How to Sow Seeds Outdoors

Many annuals can be successfully sown outdoors, directly into the garden. Just loosen the soil, work in organic matter, and rake it smooth to create a seed bed. (You can prepare an entire garden bed this way or simply rake up patches of unplanted soil in an existing garden to prepare those spots for sowing.) Gently sprinkle the seeds over the site, then lightly rake the site again, and use a fine spray from a hose or watering can to briefly water the site. Water daily in dry weather. Once seedlings have sprouted and

Quick Sowing Tip

When sowing tiny seeds in the garden, it can be difficult to keep track of where you've already sprinkled them. Make it easier by mixing the plant seed with white play sand before sowing; you'll be able to tell at a glance what ground you've covered.

are two to three inches tall, thin them to the recommended spacing (see seed packets) so each plant has room to grow.

Outdoor planting can be done almost any time of the year, although in colder climates seeds started in early fall may not develop deep enough roots to survive the winter. Generally, seed starting in spring and early summer is more successful.

To sow an entire garden of annuals, prepare the site, then use a stick to draw your design on the ground before sowing each drift.

BUYING FLOWERS TO TRANSPLANT

If you don't want to start your own plants from seed, you can buy seedlings or more mature plants and transplant them in your garden. If this is the path you choose, spend a little time up front making sure that you select healthy plants. Most garden centers try very hard to supply healthy plants in peak condition—free of disease and insect infestations—but it still pays to look plants over carefully before you buy.

A top-notch garden center will have healthy plants and informative signs and labels to help you make plant choices.

First and foremost, observe the overall degree of care plants receive at the nursery or garden center. Wilted plants, sun-scorched leaves, or bone-dry soil suggest neglect. Each time a plant wilts badly, it loses strength. If the retailer doesn't water regularly and doesn't provide shade for plants that need it, the plants will likely be in a weakened condition when you buy them. This, in turn, makes them more susceptible to disease and insect infestations. Avoid shopping where plants haven't received proper care.

When possible, buy plants early in the season, especially if you are buying from a store that only sells plants occasionally rather than at a garden center or nursery. Too often, plants arrive at such stores in healthy condition but are tended by store personnel who know nothing about plants. The result is haphazard watering and other shoddy care, resulting in sickly plants.

Do an Up-Close Inspection

Wherever you shop, look over each plant carefully for overall signs of health and proper care. Before you buy any new plant, check the following:

Leaf color. The foliage of naturally green-leaved plants should be bright green, not faded yellow or scorched bronze or brown.

Plant shape. Seedlings should be compact—short and stocky—with narrow stretches of stem between sets of leaves. Established plants should be bushy.

Roots. Ideally, a plant will have roots that fill its pot without being cramped. The best way to judge root quality is to pop a plant out of its container (or ask a salesclerk to do this) and check to see how matted the roots have become.

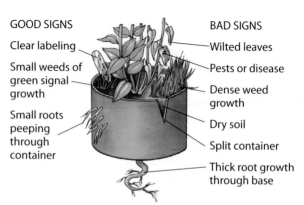

GOOD SIGNS

Clear labeling

Small weeds of green signal growth

Small roots peeping through container

BAD SIGNS

Wilted leaves

Pests or disease

Dense weed growth

Dry soil

Split container

Thick root growth through base

Looking for these signs can help you judge the health of container-grown annuals or perennials before you buy.

Soil. The potting soil should be rich and moist (and foliage perky rather than wilted). A plant that has not been getting the water it needs is already in a weakened state and may not survive the shock of transplanting. It is also more likely to fall victim to pests or disease.

Heed Specific Warning Signs

When inspecting each plant before purchase, look for insects as well as for signs pointing to infestation or disease. Obviously if

If You See:	Plant Likely Has:
Ants (which protect aphids) busily running up and down stems	Aphids
Chewed leaf edges or large holes in leaves	Caterpillars
Clouds of tiny white insects rising from the plant when you touch it	White flies
Extremely fine webs on underside of leaves	Spider mites
Grayish-white powder on leaves	Mildew
Hard, round or oval, shell-like formations on stems	Scale
Plant tips wilted, while lower stems and leaves are not	Stem borers
Chewed foliage and shiny, slimy trails on leaves	Slugs or snails
Squiggly trails in leaves	Leaf miners
Stickiness on plant stems and leaves	Mites or aphids
Stippled holes dotting leaves	Leafhoppers
Tiny, soft-bodied bugs on flower buds and growth tips	Aphids
Whitish fluff that turns sticky if pinched	Mealybugs

insects come fluttering out when you shake a plant, you should take a pass. But also check for pests on the underside of leaves and along the stem. Inspect the stem tips and flower buds, where small, pear-shaped troublemakers called aphids like to hide. Use the symptom guide on page 29 to detect other potential pest problems or poor health in plants before you buy.

TRANSPLANTING

Whether you're moving your homegrown seedlings or your purchased plants into the garden, it pays to handle them with care. Transplant stress slows growth and affects overall performance, so use the following information to ease the transition.

Harden Off Sheltered Plants

Seedlings that you grew indoors or plants that were inside a greenhouse when you bought them will need to be hardened off. That's a gardener's term for gradually getting plants used to the conditions outdoors before you transplant them into your garden, so they don't suffer shock and/or wilt. To harden off your plants, first make sure they are well watered, then set them outside in a protected spot for an hour the first day. A site on the north side of a building or under an evergreen tree is ideal. After an hour, bring the plants indoors, then take them out the second day for a longer period of time. Gradually extend their daily outdoor time over the course of a week until they're ready to spend the night outdoors. Once you've hardened your plants this way, they're ready to be bedded down in your garden.

Check the Weather

Your transplants will thank you if you check the weather forecast before bedding them in the garden. Ideally, do your transplanting on an overcast or even rainy day. Cool, cloudy, rainy weather gives your plants extra time to adjust to their new home and recover from transplanting before sunny weather returns. If cloudy weather isn't in the forecast, transplant in the evening.

Tuck Them in Beds ASAP

Container-grown plants that are bound for the garden should be hardened and transplanted as soon as the weather permits. (Don't move annuals out before temperatures warm up enough in spring, though.) Generally speaking, the longer they're in containers, the more likely they are to dry out and become pot-bound (their roots so densely matted within the pot that their growth is stunted). Weather permitting, homegrown seedlings can be hardened and transplanted into the garden after they get their first true leaves; purchased plants should be hardened and transplanted as soon as possible after you buy them. If you can't plant right away, harden off plants, keep them in light shade, and water them regularly. Follow the steps below for successful transplanting.

1. Water before you move. Thoroughly moisten the soil before sliding plants from pots. Water them the day before you transplant, or plunge the container into a pail of water to just above the pot's rim for a few minutes prior to transplanting.

2. Handle with care. To keep the root-ball intact and avoid damage to the plant, splay your fingers across the top of the pot, turn the pot upside down, and gently tap the rim to loosen the root-ball. The plant should slide out into your hand. If it doesn't, rap the rim on a solid surface before sliding it out. If pot-bound plants still resist coming out, do not try to pull them out; this can damage the stems and/or roots. Instead, carefully cut and/or peel back the sides of their plastic pots to release the plants.

To remove each plant from its pot, cradle it by splaying your fingers over the top of the pot—so the stems and leaves are between your fingers—and turn it over.

3. Loosen the roots. Gently loosen the roots to encourage them to spread out into the soil. Otherwise, they will tend to keep growing in a tight mass. Note: Take only one plant out of

If roots resist loosening with your fingers, cut up into the sides of the root ball in several places with a sharp knife or scissors, then shake the roots loose a bit more with your fingers before planting.

its pot at a time to limit how long the roots are exposed to the drying qualities of air and light.

4. Seat the plant in a good-size hole. Dig a hole that's somewhat larger in diameter than the plant's root-ball and deep enough for the plant to sit at the same depth as it did in the pot. Make a small soil mound in the center of the hole, and, as you lower the plant in, spread the loosened roots over the mound to encourage the roots to fan out as they grow.

5. Refill, and water. Refill the hole with soil, then press down on the soil around the roots to firm it. Create a rim of soil around the plant to hold in water, then water the plant deeply. As the water soaks in, it will settle the soil and remove remaining air pockets around the roots.

6. Mulch. Spread a two-inch-thick layer of mulch around the plant and under trailing foliage, but keep the mulch an inch or so away from the main stem of the plant.

7. Provide a sun hat. Protecting new transplants from direct sun helps them recover from transplanting. For best results, set overturned boxes (prop them up on one side so air can circulate) over plants, or cover plants with bushel baskets for three to four days to help them adjust.

How to Transplant Bare-Root Plants

Some perennials—especially those that arrive by mail—are sold without soil on their roots. Daylilies are commonly shipped bare root, and most perennials shipped this way can be transplanted in spring or fall. (Bare-root bearded irises, Oriental poppies, and peonies usually fare best if transplanted only in fall.) If the roots are bone-dry when you receive your shipment, there is some cause for concern. Thoroughly soak them immediately, and report any that don't show signs of new growth to the shipper. Mail-order nurseries are so experienced in packing bare-root plants that there is seldom a problem; when there is, it's usually because the shipment was somehow delayed in transit.

Ideally, you should transplant bare-root plants immediately upon receipt. If that's impossible, unpack them right away and place their roots in a container of water (do not submerge the tops) for a few hours, then repack them in their shipping material. Keep them away from wind and sun. If you can't plant within a day of their arrival, pot them up and grow them in containers until you can plant them in the garden.

Carry bare-root perennials to the garden in a bucket of water to keep the roots moist. Trim any extra-long or damaged roots with sharp scissors before planting. Inspect, trim, and transplant one plant at a time to avoid extended exposure of the

> ## When to Bed Bare-Root Plants
>
> The best time to transplant bare-root plants depends on where you live.
>
> **Northeast:** spring or early to late fall
> **Middle-Atlantic:** mid- to late fall
> **Southeast:** mid- to late fall or early spring
> **Midwest:** spring or late summer to early fall
> **Plains states:** spring or early to mid-fall
> **Rockies:** spring
> **Pacific Northwest:** early spring or fall
> **California:** early spring or mid- to late fall
> **Southwest:** early to mid-spring

roots to air and sun. For each plant, dig a hole large enough to allow you to spread the roots out in all directions. Build a cone of soil in the center of the hole on which to set the plant so that it will sit at the same soil depth in the garden as it was in the nursery; look for the soil line on the stem as a guide. Follow the directions that accompany the shipment if the plants you receive have no stems or top growth to serve as indicators. Care for the new bare-root transplants as you would container-grown ones.

Managing and Enjoying Your Flowers

Once your flowers are planted in the garden, get in the habit of visiting them daily. You'll find that by paying attention, you can easily and quickly identify and remedy problems and even prevent some in the first place. It's this kind of attention and basic care that turns a good garden into a great one—one that you can enjoy to the fullest.

KEEPING PLANTS HAPPY AND HEALTHY

Keeping easy-to-grow annuals like zinnias healthy is simple. Once they're planted in a good site in good soil, all they need is regular watering and deadheading.

On your daily garden visits, keep an eye out for plants that need watering, weeds that are emerging, spots that need additional mulch, and other issues you can address before they get out of hand. Use the information in this section to help you keep all of your flowers thriving.

Watering the Garden

Annuals require regular watering throughout their short lives, and newly planted perennials need regular watering during the first season they're in the ground whenever nature doesn't supply enough rain. After that, most perennials can sustain themselves without being watered, except during exceptionally dry spells.

So how do you judge when to water and how much water to give? You can install a rain gauge to monitor how much moisture plants receive from rainfall. But whether you use a rain gauge or not, you should get in the habit of testing soil moisture by poking your finger two to three inches into the ground to feel how moist or dry it is. Taking a pinch from the surface isn't good enough; you need to know what conditions are like down in the root zone. Inexperienced gardeners should check soil moisture any day that there is little or no rainfall. Over time, you'll only need to check when you suspect the soil may be turning dry. Remember, it's always better to check too often than not often enough. Don't wait until drooping plants indicate that the soil is parched. And keep in mind that flowers growing under trees and shrubs dry out more quickly than plants without competition.

With a soaker hose, water slowly seeps into the soil—allowing deep, thorough watering and minimizing waste due to runoff and evaporation. Lay the soaker hose(s) through your garden bed early in the season (leaving the end that connects to a regular hose or spigot near the outside edge of the bed), and cover it with mulch. When it's time to water, connect it to the regular hose or spigot, and turn on the water.

When you do need to water, always water deeply to encourage deep root growth. If only the top inch or two is moistened, the plants' roots will cluster near the surface. Surface soil dries out more rapidly than deeper soil, and when it does, shallow-rooted plants quickly wilt. Deep watering also wastes less water. Whenever you water, check to see that the water has seeped down to a depth of six to eight inches by sticking your finger down into the soil.

Mulching

Experienced gardeners keep their soil covered with mulch for a variety of reasons. Mulch greatly reduces the need for weeding by preventing many weeds from ever sprouting. It also protects soil

from wind and rain erosion and moisture evaporation; keeps the soil cool in summer; and gives the garden a neat, cared-for appearance.

Spread two inches of mulch over the garden soil right after planting, and replenish it as needed. As you spread it, take care to lift trailing foliage so it lies on top of the mulch, but be sure to keep the mulch an inch or two away from the main stem or crown of the plant. This helps prevent disease. Use any mulch material that's readily available and inexpensive in your area: shredded bark, chopped leaves, peanut shells,

Keeping a flower garden mulched helps to hold moisture in the soil and helps to keep the soil healthy while eliminating most weeds.

buckwheat or cocoa bean hulls, pine needles, or wood chips.

If you are sowing seed outdoors, wait to spread mulch until after the seeds have germinated and the resulting seedlings are three or more inches tall. Otherwise, the mulch can smother the tiny seedlings.

Keeping Weeds at Bay

Weed seeds are quick to germinate, and they grow rapidly. That's why keeping a garden mulched is so important. But even if you

Weed When It's Wet

After a substantial rain, when the soil is wet, get out your trowel or dandelion fork, kneel next to the garden bed, and spend some time removing dandelions and other perennial weeds. The roots of all weeds slip out of the soil more easily when it's wet.

mulch, be vigilant about weeds, especially in newly turned beds. As soon as tilling or digging brings weed seeds to within an inch of the soil surface, they'll begin to sprout. So immediately after turning and mulching a new bed—and then once a day for the two or more weeks until you plant—stir up the top inch of soil with an oscillating (stirrup) or scuffle hoe (which won't disturb the mulch layer much) or a cultivator. Leave the lower soil undisturbed, and be sure to remulch any areas left bare in the process. Repeat this practice once every three days after you plant as well. This will upend any young weeds that do manage to sprout, so they'll dry out and die from exposure to sunlight and air.

Feeding Your Flowers

If you add plenty of compost and other organic matter to your soil at planting time—and get in the habit of digging in more every time you plant or disturb the soil—your flowers will probably do just fine without any supplemental fertilizer. If your flowers haven't been performing as well as they should, however, consider applying a slow-release, organic fertilizer in late fall or during the following spring before growth begins. A good time to fertilize is just before you refresh the mulch on the beds.

Choose a balanced granular fertilizer: The three numbers on the front of the bag should be the same (10–10–10, for example). Opt for an organic fertilizer, because inorganic, or chemical, fertilizers add salts to the soil that drive away beneficial soil organisms such as earthworms. To apply fertilizer, read the package directions to determine the recommended dose, then sprinkle it over the root zone of each plant. Avoid getting granules on leaves. Ideally, apply fertilizer just before a rainfall or watering, which will start the feeding process.

Making Compost

Called gardener's gold, compost is the best fertilizer for your flowers. Make it the lazy way by piling layers of leaves, kitchen waste, and other organic matter in an inconspicuous corner of your yard. An ideal blend would consist of equal amounts soft, or green, material (manure and fresh leaves or grass, for example) and brown, or hard, material (dead leaves and chopped twigs). If you prefer, keep these ingredients neatly contained in a wooden-slat or wire-mesh bin. Let them sit for about a year, and your compost will be ready. Nature's recyclers will take organic matter no matter how it is presented and turn it into rich, dark compost. It just takes longer in an untended pile.

To supply food for immediate use by newly planted bedding annuals, use a watering can to pour a weak solution of water-soluble organic fertilizer (such as fish emulsion) directly around each plant. Thereafter, sprinkling granular plant food around each plant at two-week intervals should carry annuals through the rest of the summer.

A few simple grooming tasks—such as staking tall, heavy-blossomed plants like these delphiniums—can keep your garden looking good.

KEEPING PLANTS LOOKING THEIR BEST

Annuals and perennials benefit from simple grooming techniques, such as pinching, deadheading, and staking. Keep up with these tasks on your daily rambles through the garden, and they'll never become overwhelming.

Pinching and Shearing

Pinching and shearing are grooming techniques that, timed properly, encourage plants to branch out and grow fuller. Fall-blooming flowers such as chrysanthemums, for example, benefit from either technique. Pinching or shearing will result in more flowers and denser growth come fall. But in general, you should only cut back fall-blooming plants before about July fourth, so the flowers have enough time to form before the first frost.

Shearing consists of using a sharp-bladed implement to cut back the entire top of a plant by several inches. This encourages the plant to send out, and direct energy to, more side branches.

Pinching involves removing just the tip of an individual stem, usually using your fingers. You simply pinch or snap off the last inch or so of the main growing tip. This will redirect the plant's energy from this single shoot to numerous latent side buds (a latent growth bud is located at each node, which is the point on the stem where a leaf is attached). Several days after pinching, you'll see several small shoots pushing out from the remaining stem. These will grow into a cluster of stems to replace the original single stem. The result will be a shorter, stockier, fuller plant that looks neater and has more branches capable of producing flowers. (Shearing has similar effects.) A second pinching can be done two weeks after the first for an even fuller plant, if desired.

For young plants, the best time to pinch out growth tips is when you're transplanting them into the garden. They're at a good stage of growth, and this type of pruning will help them withstand the stress of transplanting. For plants grown from seed sown directly in the garden, pinching should be done when the seedlings are three to four inches tall.

Deadheading

In most cases, once your plants begin blooming, you'll want to deadhead them—remove spent flowers—promptly. To do so, cut off spent blooms just above the first side bud that's beginning to grow. If no active side bud is visible, cut back to a side branch. Make a clean cut with a sharp-bladed knife or scissors; ragged cuts take much longer to heal.

Deadheading keeps the garden looking neat and redirects the energy that plants would otherwise spend producing seed into new flowers and growth instead.

Staking Flowers

Most flowers don't require staking, but plants with heavy flower clusters, especially on tall, slender stems, may flop over in wind and rain. Ideally, install stakes before plants flop, because it is easier to achieve an attractive, natural effect.

Single staking. Tie stems to a stake that is firmly anchored in the soil. First tie the string around the stake with a half-granny knot, allowing an inch or more of slack between the stake and the plant stem. Then tie a full-granny knot around the stem. As the plant grows taller, add ties further up on the stake, six to eight inches apart. The topmost tie should be located at the base of the flower spike.

Stake corrals. To support clumps, insert stakes around the plant. Tie a

L-shaped metal stakes, available at garden centers, can often be used in place of straight stakes and string to corral clumps of flowers..

string to the first stake, then wrap it one turn around each of the other stakes along the perimeter and back to the starter stake. For a large clump, run string diagonally across the clump for more support. Several tiers of string spaced four to six inches apart may be needed for tall plants.

DIVIDING PERENNIALS

Perennials—especially those that spread quickly—need to be dug up and divided every few years. Division helps keep perennials within bounds and gives you the chance to remove older, less vital portions of each clump. A natural by-product of this process is additional plants, which you can replant in your own garden or share with friends.

Perennials can be divided by lifting an entire clump and cutting it apart or by taking pieces away from the clump's outer edges—separating the pieces from the main plant by cutting through the crown with a knife or sharp-bladed spade.

Timing

Except in the South, the best time to divide most perennials is early spring. But you should wait to divide early-spring bloomers until right after they're done flowering. And there are a few plants—peonies, irises, and Oriental poppies—that, despite being summer bloomers, do better if they're divided after they've finished flowering and begun to change color. In the South, fall is a better time to divide all perennials except Oriental poppies.

Separating Roots

The simplest way to divide clumps is by pulling them apart with your hands or by slicing off a portion from the outside edge of the clump with a trowel or spade. Cut clumps into several large

pieces rather than into many very small ones; this will provide fewer plants, but they'll be healthier and more likely to bloom the first season after division.

For plants with tight, dense clumps of roots, use two spading forks to divide them. Once you've lifted the clump out of the ground, stick the forks through it back-to-back. By pushing outward on the fork handles, it's usually possible to pry the clump apart. Some clumps hold together so tenaciously, however, that hacking them into chunks with a heavy knife, cleaver, or hatchet is the only alternative. Don't be afraid you'll harm the plant—those that are this tough won't be fazed by such treatment!

Whichever method you choose, try to keep as many of the roots intact as possible and to have some roots and some foliage in each division. Trim back excess top foliage to balance the loss of feeder roots that takes place when the plants are dug up and torn apart. Avoid the impulse to get as many separate clumps as possible: Larger clumps will thrive, while small divisions are likely to struggle and grow very slowly.

Always plant the new divisions at the same depth they were growing before you dug up the original clump. Firm the soil

Some perennials (bearded irises, for example) have large, fleshy underground stems called rhizomes. To divide these, dig up the entire rhizome clump, and shake out the dirt. Then use a sharp knife to cleanly cut the rhizome into smaller clumps containing three or more buds. Discard any pieces of rhizome that appear rotted or are infested with boring insects. Let the pieces air dry for about an hour before replanting, so the wounds can seal over.

around each new plant, and water well to help settle the soil closely around the roots. Be sure to deeply water new divisions as needed during their first weeks in the garden.

MANAGING PESTS AND DISEASE

Growing healthy plants is the first step toward keeping pests and disease at bay. That's because vigorous plants are better able to ward off attacks by pests and pathogens. Here are a few basic steps you can take to keep plants healthy and free of invaders.

Plants that are healthy and thriving are better able to shrug off pest and disease problems than ones that are struggling to survive.

Build good soil. Soil that drains well is very important, because soggy roots almost always lead to rot, although there are some plants that thrive with wet feet. Adding organic matter to soil improves drainage. It also helps build populations of soil organisms that actually help protect plants from pests and disease.

Avoid overcrowding. Plants with enough space to grow and reach maturity compete less with their neighbors for sunlight, water, and nutrients, plus they receive plenty of fresh air. Good air circulation discourages diseases such as powdery mildew and keeps plants healthier.

Handle plants gently. Use a sharp knife or clippers for grooming and cutting, and avoid pulling or tearing at stems. Clean cuts heal faster, while torn stems admit disease organisms. Also avoid working among plants when they are wet, which can encourage the spread of plant diseases.

Attract beneficials.
Interspersing flowering plants
throughout your landscape
helps draw ladybugs, spiders,
lacewings, parasitic wasps, and
other beneficial insects that
prey on or lay their eggs in
plant-eating pests. The flowers

provide adult beneficials with shelter (mulch also provides shelter
for certain beneficials), nectar and pollen to eat, and places to lay
their eggs. Their immature offspring, in turn, gorge themselves on
plant pests. To avoid cutting down beneficials in your garden,
avoid broad-spectrum pesticides, which kill good bugs and bad.

Simple Controls for Common Pests

Surprisingly, the vast majority of insects you'll see in your garden
are beneficial or benign and not pests, so you should try to
identify insects before you decide to kill them. You can take
samples to your local cooperative extension service, to Master
Gardener events, or to your local nursery for help with identifica-
tion as well as recommendations for control. Here are some
simple solutions to common pest problems:

Hose off aphids and spider mites. Control both these pests
by blasting them off plants with a strong stream of water from
the hose. Aphids are pinhead-size insects that cluster on the
underside of leaves. Spider mites are barely visible, eight-legged
arachnids that spin webs under leaves and over stem tips.

Trap slugs. Slugs (and snails) are voracious plant eaters that
can consume entire seedlings or chew large holes in leaves. They
thrive where the soil is damp, spending sunny days under rocks,
logs, or mulch and coming out to eat when it's rainy or cool and
dark. Kill existing slugs with beer traps: Bury an empty plastic
margarine tub in the garden so the tub's rim is level with the soil
surface. Fill the container with beer (any kind will do), and leave
it overnight. Slugs, which are attracted to beer, will crawl in and

drown. Empty the tub every day or two and refill with beer until it comes through the night slugfree.

Use cutworm collars on seedlings. When seedlings break through the garden soil or when you transfer transplants to the garden, protect them from cutworms by placing a three- to four-inch-high section of a toilet paper tube around each plant's stem. This prevents cutworms from devouring entire seedlings or attacking plants at night and cutting them off at ground level.

USING YOUR FLOWERS

Without doubt, your garden will offer you countless hours of pleasure as you tend your annuals and perennials and gaze out at them through the kitchen window. To extend that enjoyment, bring fresh bouquets of cut flowers indoors and try drying bunches of blooms to display in your home in winter.

Large drifts of a single flower, such as this 'Tiger Eye' hybrid rudbeckia, provide a convenient, summer-long source of flowers for cutting.

Flowers for Cutting

If you love bringing fresh flowers indoors but don't want to disrupt your carefully planned outdoor flower display, consider planting extra flowers for cutting. You can either plant flowers for cutting in large drifts within your garden landscape, so that removing a few won't hurt the overall look of the garden, or you can grow a special cutting garden. Prepare the soil as you would for any flower garden, then just sow the flowers in rows.

To ensure a bountiful supply of indoor bouquets without diminishing the flowers in your landscape, devote part of your yard to growing flowers for cutting.

Ideally, when planting flowers for cutting, look for seeds in single-color or color-blend packets rather than mixing seeds from many different flowers. Buying individual packets lets you pick colors separately and also makes it easier to organize and care for your flowers.

When you cut flowers, use a sharp knife and cut on a slant to maximize the transfer of water up into the stem once they're in a vase. Place the flowers in water as soon as you cut them, and bring them indoors promptly. Remove the leaves from the lower portion of each stem, then put the flowers into a tall container of fresh water. Set the container in a cool, dark spot until you are ready to arrange them.

Drying & Pressing Annuals

Dried bouquets are expensive to buy but easy and inexpensive to grow yourself. You can include flowers for drying in your beds and borders, or you can plant them in a separate area and grow them in rows for easy care and harvesting.

Hanging is the easiest way to dry flowers. Start by cutting flowers when they are at the peak of their maturity. Remove most of the leaves from the stems, and use elastic bands to fasten six to eight stems together to form small bundles. Large, thick-stemmed flowers—sunflowers or

---

Flowers for Cutting

All of the flowers listed below make excellent additions to bouquets.

- Celosia
- Coreopsis
- Cosmos
- Dahlias
- Echinaceas
- Lavender
- Marigolds
- Phlox
- Rudbeckias
- Salvias
- Shasta daisies
- Snapdragons
- Stokesia
- Sunflowers
- Zinnias

Strawflowers are prized for their double daisylike flowers, which have a papery texture even when fresh. Their stems are extremely brittle, so handle them with care, or use florist wire to reinforce them.

roses, for example—should be hung individually.

Hang bundles upside-down in a dry, well-ventilated area that is out of direct sun. A well-ventilated attic or garage works fine, but flowers will also dry if hung in a shady screened-in porch or even from a dining-room ceiling, provided the humidity is low and there is good air circulation. Leave enough space between bundles to allow for good air circulation. The flowers will dry in two to three weeks.

Hang small bunches of flowers in a dry, well-ventilated area away from direct sun. You can use brown bags to protect them from dust.

CONTAINER GARDENING

Growing flowers in containers is a fun, creative, and easy way to garden, whether you want to add single spots of color to a patio or plant an entire grouping of containers. You can even garden in

When filling containers, place pieces of broken pottery in the bottom to allow water to drain while keeping the soil in. Use a layer of foam packing "peanuts" or foam chunks at the bottom if you are concerned about the overall weight of the filled container.

containers on a rooftop, a high-rise balcony, a raised deck, a fire escape, or a yard covered with concrete. Use the following suggestions to select and plant a successful container garden.

Choose your containers. All that's essential is that the container be capable of holding soil and allowing excess water to drain away. Large containers are generally better than small ones because the soil in them dries out more slowly and plants' roots don't overheat as quickly. Beyond that, the sky is the limit. Choose from terra cotta, ceramic, plastic, lightweight resin, and wood containers. (If you are gardening on a wooden deck or balcony, pay attention to the overall weight of the container when it's filled with moist soil.) And don't forget to consider hanging baskets or window boxes.

Fill containers generously. Use commercial or homemade potting mix to fill them. Plant a single annual per pot, or create a more lavish display by filling each container with several annuals. When combining plants in a container, include different flower colors and foliage textures to add interest. Ideally, use one eye-catching plant as a focal point, and blend others in around it.

Care for containers regularly. A container garden needs daily attention. Check soil moisture every evening. When the weather is dry and windy, check it morning and evening. To determine if plants need watering, rub a pinch of soil between your thumb and finger. If the soil feels at all dry to the touch, water. On the other hand,

---

Annuals for Containers

A great many annuals can thrive in a container garden. These are some of the best:

❦ Begonias	❦ Marigolds
❦ Coleus	❦ Nasturtiums
❦ Geraniums	❦ Pansies
❦ Impatiens	❦ Petunias

---

the soil should not be constantly soaking wet, because the plants will drown. When watering, be sure water reaches all of the soil in the container: Fill the planter to the rim with water several times, allowing it to soak in completely. If no water comes out of the drainage holes, fill again. Repeat this process until water starts to drip from the bottom of the container.

Also pinch and deadhead potted plants regularly to keep them blooming and looking their best. Fertilize every ten days with liquid fertilizer; dilute it to the recommended strength for containers, as directed on the label.

Change the display. Containers are portable, so don't hesitate to move them around the garden! Bring new containers to prime spots as they begin to flower, and retire or rest pots that have finished flowering. Also, don't hesitate to dig up a plant that's not performing well or has finished flowering and replace it with something else.

PUTTING THE GARDEN TO BED

As the days shorten and winter approaches, the gardening season draws to a close. It's the time to clean and store your gardening tools and get garden beds ready for winter. Plan time for these winter chores.

Perennials for Containers

Perennials—both hardy and tender—make handsome container plants. Keeping tender plants in pots makes it especially easy to move them indoors over the winter. Try some of these perennial favorites:

- Chrysanthemums
- Daylilies
- Ferns
- Gaillardias
- Hostas
- Lavender
- Rudbeckias
- Salvias
- Scabiosa
- Sedums
- Shasta daisies

Keep in mind that large pots, like the ones shown here holding geraniums, require less frequent watering than small pots do.

Take care of tools. Clean dirt off tools and coat metal parts with a thin layer of light oil to protect them from rust. Sand and revarnish wooden handles. Sharpen shovels, spades, and other tools. Drain and roll up hoses.

Test the soil. If you suspect your soil isn't what it could be, fall is a great time to take soil samples and get them tested. You can add amendments in fall or winter and be ready to start gardening again come spring.

Cut back annuals. Once frost hits, cut back annuals and add those that haven't gone to seed to your compost pile.

Echinaceas (purple coneflowers) and rudbeckias bear seeds that help feed birds during the winter months.

Ease perennials into winter. As the season comes to an end, stop fertilizing perennials. Stop deadheading, too; let a few flowers set seed. Once frost hits the tops of the plants, you can cut them back. But don't cut back plants with evergreen leaves or seed-setting plants like echinaceas and rudbeckias that help feed birds during the winter months. Cut these back in early spring.

Dig up and store tender perennials. Cannas, four-o'clocks, and dahlias all have fleshy roots that can be dug up in fall and stored indoors over the winter. Also dig up tender bulbs like gladioli, tuberous begonias, and caladiums for winter storage indoors. Although you can treat all these plants as if they were annuals by simply discarding them each fall and buying new ones in spring, there's no need, because overwintering is so easy. After frost hits the tops of the plants, dig them up and leave them in the sun for a few hours. Remove the dead tops and any loose soil and feeder roots from the root area. Then store them in barely moist vermiculite in boxes set in a cool (40°F), dark spot for the winter. Store bulbs and bulblike corms loosely in brown-paper sacks or open-weave bags in a dark, cool area. Be sure to check overwintered plants regularly for rot or shriveled, dry tubers. Discard rooted growth, and sprinkle shriveled roots with water to rehydrate them.

Take time to plant bulbs. Fall is the time to plant most spring-blooming bulbs, including daffodils, crocuses, and tulips. By spending a few warm afternoons planting bulbs, you can ensure a gorgeous display come spring.

Raising Cuttings over Winter

Weeks before frost threatens, think about taking and rooting cuttings to avoid having to bring large tender plants inside for the winter. To take cuttings, use a sharp knife or clippers to cut just below a leaf node (the point on the stem where a leaf is attached). Keep cuttings moist in a plastic bag or in water until you are ready to pot them up. To root them, dip the cut end of the stems in rooting hormone and stick them—cut end down—into pots filled with a moistened mix of half perlite and half vermiculite. Cover with clear plastic, and place under grow lights. Providing bottom heat with a warming mat (available at garden centers) or by placing the container atop the refrigerator, will speed rooting. Once roots have formed, move plants to pots filled with ordinary potting soil.

You can overwinter many tender perennials, including coleus, geraniums, and begonias, by taking cuttings.

Dip the cut tip of the stem in rooting hormone. Then, before sticking the tip into the potting mix, use a pencil to make a hole for it, so the hormone doesn't get rubbed off as it goes in.

Cover pots or trays of cuttings with a plastic bag or a tent made from a dry-cleaner bag to hold in moisture until roots form in several weeks.

Easy Garden Flowers

Deciding what flowers to grow is one of the most enjoyable aspects of gardening, whether you do it while browsing through a catalog, turning the pages of a book, or spinning a seed rack at your local garden center. In this chapter, you'll find information on some of the best flowers you can grow. In addition to text, the flower profiles include helpful icons—their meanings are listed below—to provide you with even more information on plant features and growing requirements.

 Good for cut-flower bouquets

 Good for drying

 Suitable for containers

 Fragrant flowers or foliage

 Handsome foliage

 Attracts butterflies, beneficial insects, moths, or hummingbirds

 Resents transplanting; sow in individual pots and handle with care, or sow directly outdoors

 Sow seeds indoors at 65° to 70°F, 6 to 8 weeks before last spring frost date in your area, and transplant outdoors after soil has warmed and all danger of frost has passed

 Sow seeds in winter or very early spring, mulch pots with gravel, and set outdoors in a protected spot for germination in spring or summer

 Plants self-sow

 Don't cover seeds when sowing; they require light to germinate

Achillea

Achillea species
Perennial
Hardiness: Zones 3 to 8

Also called yarrows, achilleas grow 1 to 4 feet high, blooming from June until frost. Flowers are small and arranged in flat heads on top of stout stems. Blooms come in yellow, pink, apricot, red, white, or violet. The foliage is finely cut, with a ferny texture.

How to grow: Yarrows tolerate drought and are suitable for any garden soil that has good drainage. Plants perform best in full sun, although they will put up with a bit of shade. Propagate by division in spring or fall or by sowing seeds.

Uses: Yarrows are excellent in garden borders and in mass plantings.

Selections: Many hybrids are available in a range of rich colors. 'Summer Wine' bears pink buds that open to dark pink flowers on 2-foot-tall stems. 'Coronation Gold' bears deep yellow flowers.

Ageratum

Ageratum houstonianum
Annual

These fluffy flowers bloom continuously from summer to fall in shades of blue-lavender, white, or pink. Use compact, mounding types, 6 to 10 inches high, in beds; use 12- to 15-inch-tall selections for cut flowers.

How to grow: Grow in any well-drained soil in full sun or partial shade. Occasional deadheading improves performance. Plants need ample water to ensure leaves never wilt. Start seeds indoors and move plants outdoors after all chance of frost has passed, since ageratums are especially frost sensitive. Cover seeds very lightly; they need some light to germinate well. Seeds germinate in 5 to 8 days at 70°F.

Uses: Plant in the front of borders and beds or in containers.

Selections: Popular blue varieties include 8-inch 'Blue Danube' and 12- to 15-inch 'Blue Blazer'.

Alyssum, Sweet

Lobularia maritima
Annual

Sweet alyssum bears clusters of tiny, fragrant flowers for months on end. Plants grow only a few inches high but spread as much as 1 foot in diameter. Flowers come in white as well as pink, lavender, or violet.

How to grow: Alyssum grows best in full sun in cool weather but tolerates partial shade. In mild climates, sow in fall for blooms in winter. Otherwise, sow seeds outdoors in spring as soon as the soil is no longer frozen, or sow seeds indoors 4 to 6 weeks earlier and move small plants to the garden. Seeds germinate in 7 to 14 days at 65° to 70°F.

Uses: Use alyssum for edging beds and borders, in rock gardens, or between paving stones.

Selections: 'Carpet of Snow' is a popular white. 'Royal Carpet' bears violet purple blooms.

Amaranthus

Amaranthus species
Annual

Fast-growing amaranths tolerate poor soil, heat, and drought. *A. tricolor,* commonly called Joseph's-coat, is 3 to 5 feet tall and produces foliage in yellow, red, orange, and green. *A. caudatus* is often called tassel flower for its cascading ropelike blooms.

How to grow: Give amaranths full sun and well-drained soil. Wet soil and poor drainage cause root rot and death. Start seeds indoors, or sow directly outdoors, but don't sow or move plants outdoors until all chance of frost has passed. Germination takes 7 days at 70° to 75°F.

Uses: Use amaranths in beds and borders. Also use *A. caudatus* in containers and for cutting.

Selections: *A. tricolor* 'Flaming Fountains' has long, willowy, crimson leaves. *A. caudatus* 'Love-Lies-Bleeding' bears drooping spikes of blood-red flowers.

Aster, China

Callistephus chinensis
Annual

Popular China asters produce single, semidouble, and double flowers on 1- to 2-foot-tall plants. Flowers come in shades of white, purple, pink, yellow, blue, or red. Bloom times differ, with early, mid-, and late-summer varieties. For a continuous show, use different varieties and/or stagger sowing dates.

How to grow: China asters need full sun, rich soil, and ample water. Select disease-resistant cultivars when you buy seeds or plants. Sow seeds indoors or sow outdoors after the last spring frost date. Germination takes 10 to 20 days at 70°F. Plants will bloom only 3 to 4 weeks, so sow new crops every 10 days.

Uses: Use China asters in beds and borders or in cutting gardens.

Selections: Many mixes are available in a range of colors. 'Totem Pole' produces 4-inch-wide double flowers.

Astilbe

Astilbe species
Perennial
Hardiness: Zones 4 to 8

Grown for their handsome fernlike foliage and showy plumes of tiny flowers, astilbes come in white, pink, lavender, or cranberry. Bloom time varies, with selections flowering anytime from late spring to late summer. Each plant blooms for about 3 weeks, but foliage looks great for the duration of the growing season. Heights vary from 12 to 40 inches.

How to grow: Give astilbes a spot in partial shade, especially in the southern parts of the country. In areas with cool summers, they grow in full sun. Plants require rich, moist soil. To propagate, divide clumps in early spring or sow seeds outdoors in pots.

Uses: Use astilbes in beds and borders. They can also be massed as ground covers.

Selections: 'Snowcap' has large white blooms. 'Sprite' makes a good ground cover.

Begonia

Begonia species
Annual/Tender Perennial
Hardiness: Zones 8 to 10

Handsome leaves and nonstop flowers from early summer to fall frost make begonias a garden favorite. Most bear blooms in white or shades of pink, rose, or red. Popular wax begonias are mounding 8- to 10-inch-high plants. Other garden types are taller, growing to about 15 inches. Leaves come in green or shades of maroon and bronze.

How to grow: Most begonias do well in partial shade to shade and rich, moist, well-drained soil. Wax begonias also grow in full sun, except in hot climates. Start from seed or buy plants. Sow the dustlike seeds in winter, following seed packet directions carefully.

Uses: Use in summer annual borders, edging, and containers.

Selections: Many colors and forms of wax begonia are available. Also look for selections with dramatic wing-shaped leaves or green-and-white variegated foliage.

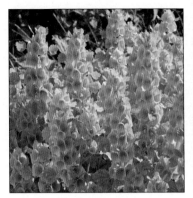

Bells of Ireland

Moluccella laevis
Annual

Bells of Ireland produce dramatic 3-foot-tall spires of large, showy green bells (or calyxes), each hiding tiny white or pinkish true flowers inside. The flowers are fragrant.

How to grow: Give plants full sun or partial shade and average, well-drained soil. In Zones 3 to 6, sow seeds outdoors 2 to 3 weeks before the last spring frost date. From Zone 7 south, sow in fall for spring germination. Or sow indoors in individual pots 8 to 10 weeks before the last spring frost, and store pots for 2 weeks in the refrigerator before germinating them at 55°F, which takes 1 to 4 weeks. Stake plants, or locate in a spot protected from wind.

Uses: Grow bells of Ireland in beds or borders and in cutting gardens.

Selections: 'Pixie Bells' grows 2 feet tall and seldom needs staking.

Campanula

Campanula species
Perennials, Biennials
Hardiness: Zones 3 to 7

Campanulas, or bellflowers, vary widely in size, shape, and plant form. Perennials range from 10 inches to several feet in height. Plants commonly bear cup-shaped or starry flowers in shades of blue, lavender, or white. They bloom from late spring into early summer.

How to grow: Most need rich, moist, well-drained soil. Give them partial shade except where summers are cool. Divide plants every few years to propagate and keep them vigorous.

Uses: Use bellflowers in beds and borders, rock gardens, and shade or wild gardens.

Selections: *C. carpatica* and *C. poscharskyana* 'Blue Waterfall' are low growers for edging or containers. *C. persicifolia,* peach-leaved bellflower, bears white or blue flowers on 3-foot-tall stems and is an excellent cut flower. Canterbury bells *(C. medium)* is a popular 1- to 3-foot-tall biennial.

Chrysanthemum

Leucanthemum species
Annuals, Perennials
Hardiness: Zones 3 to 9

Popular fall-blooming chrysanthemums, or "mums," and Shasta daisies belong to this highly variable clan. Showy flowers range from single daisies to fully double blooms. Leaves are typically divided and often aromatic. Shasta daisies bloom in summer and range from 1 to 3 feet tall.

How to grow: Give plants full sun and average to rich, well-drained, evenly moist soil. Pinch back the stems of late-blooming chrysanthemums several times until midsummer to promote bushy growth and more flowers. Propagate by division or cuttings. Some can be grown from seed.

Uses: Add Shasta daisies to summer gardens, and use mums to dress up fall flowerbeds.

Selections: Shasta daisy 'Alaska' bears 3-inch blooms. 'Snow Lady' is a vigorous summer bloomer. Chrysanthemum 'Sheffield Pink' produces its flowers in late fall.

Celosia

Celosia argentea
Annual

These heat- and humidity-loving annuals are grown for either plumelike flowers or crested blooms shaped like a rooster's comb. Flowers come in shades of yellow, gold, red, pink, orange, or wine. Leaves are green or red-burgundy. Plants range from 6 to 36 inches tall.

How to grow: Plant in full sun in average to rich, well-drained soil. Sow seeds indoors in individual pots 6 to 8 weeks before the last spring frost date. Darkness aids germination, so cover the seeds. Transplant to the garden 2 weeks after the last frost date, or sow seeds outdoors after danger of frost has passed. Seeds germinate in 10 days at 70° to 75°F.

Uses: Use celosias in beds, borders, or container combinations.

Selections: Many cultivars are available. 'Fresh Look Red' is an award winner with red flowers. 'Red Velvet' has red crested heads.

Coleus

Solenostemon scutellarioides
Annual/Tender Perennial
Hardiness: Zones 10 to 11

Coleus are grown for their lovely leaves, banded and veined with multiple colors—such as purple, lime, red, brown, white, and copper—in various lacy or plain shapes. Leaves range from 1 to 8 inches long; plants are 6 to 36 inches tall.

How to grow: Grow coleus in moist, rich soil in partial shade. Protect plants from frost and drought. Pinch back tips for bushiness. Remove flower spikes when they appear. Sow seeds indoors 10 to 12 weeks before the last spring frost date; germination takes 10 to 12 days at 72°F. Or propagate by rooting cuttings. As tender perennials, coleus can be overwintered indoors.

Uses: Use plants in containers, bedding designs, and borders.

Selections: Many color patterns are available. 'Wizard Mix' produces a good range of colors and patterns from seed.

Columbine

Aquilegia species
Perennial
Hardiness: Zones 3 to 8

These hummingbird favorites have a long blooming season. Spurred flowers with complex form bloom on wiry stems that float above a rosette of blue-green leaves. Flowers come in red, yellow, blue, white, pink, or purple. Many selections bear two-toned flowers. Double-flowered types are available, too.

How to grow: Give columbines fertile, well-drained soil and full sun or partial shade. Many only live for a few years, so allow a few plants to self-sow for continued stock. To propagate, sow seeds in pots set outdoors. Seed from hybrids will not yield seedlings that resemble the parents.

Uses: Columbines are excellent in beds and borders.

Selections: Many seed mixes are available. 'Songbird Mix' blooms are white with pink or purple. Wild columbine *(A. canadensis)* features red and yellow blooms.

Coreopsis

Coreopsis species
Annuals, Perennials
Hardiness: Zones 4 to 9

Sporting bright daisylike flowers on wiry stems, coreopsis bear single or double flowers on 9- to 36-inch-tall plants, depending on the species and cultivar. Plants bear flowers in shades of yellow, orange, pink, or white and have lance-shape, oval, or threadlike leaves.

How to grow: Give these easy-care plants full sun and almost any well-drained garden soil. Plants are drought resistant and an outstanding choice for hot, difficult places. Sow seeds indoors. Deadheading keeps plants blooming. Divide perennials every few years to keep them healthy.

Uses: Use coreopsis in beds and borders, containers, and wild gardens.

Selections: *C. verticillata* 'Moonbeam' has pale yellow daisies, and 'Zagreb' has deep yellow ones. 'Early Sunrise' blooms the first year from seed and produces double yellow flowers.

Cosmos

Cosmos species
Annual

Fast-growing cosmos bear daisylike, 3- to 4-inch-wide flowers. Gardeners grow two species: *C.bipinnatus*, which ranges from 2 to 4 feet tall and bears flowers in shades of pink, red, white, or lavender, and *C. sulphureus*, which grows 1 to 3 feet tall and produces orange, red, or yellow blooms. Foliage is feathery.

How to grow: Plants do best in full sun but tolerate partial shade. Give them poor to average, well-drained soil. Sow seed outdoors after spring frost danger has passed or indoors 4 weeks before the last frost date. Germination takes 3 to 7 days at 70° to 75°F.

Uses: Use in beds, borders, and informal meadow gardens.

Selections: Many selections are available. *C. bipinnatus* 'Sea Shells' features flowers with pretty rolled petals. 'Bright Lights Mix' yields semidouble flowers in yellow, orange, gold, and red.

Dahlia

Dahlia hybrids
Annual/Tender Perennial
Hardiness: Zones 8 to 11

Bearing flowers ranging from dinner-plate-size blooms down to midget pompoms only 2 inches in diameter, dahlias show as much diversity as any summer flowering plant. Blooms appear from summer to frost and come in every color except blue.

How to grow: Give dahlias full sun and rich, moist, well-drained soil. Plant outdoors after danger of frost has passed. Full-size dahlias reach 6 feet tall and need staking. Dwarf types are 12 to 18 inches tall and can sprawl. Grow dahlias from clumps of tuberous roots, or sow seeds indoors. Their tuberous roots may be dug in fall, stored indoors over winter, and replanted in spring.

Uses: Full-size dahlias are useful at the back of borders. Dwarf types work well as edging or in containers.

Selections: Dozens of cultivars are available. Pick your favorites!

Daylily

Hemerocallis species
Perennial
Hardiness: Zones 3 to 9

Daylilies bear trumpet-shape flowers, each one lasting only a day, but most plants produce hundreds of blooms over the course of a season. Flowers come in orange, yellow, cream, peach, lavender, or wine-red, plus bicolor. Plants have fleshy roots, range from 2 to more than 4 feet tall, and produce clumps of strap-shape leaves.

How to grow: Give daylilies full sun and average, well-drained soil. They tolerate drought and damp soil. Plants benefit from partial shade in the South. Divide plants every few years. Propagate by division in spring or fall.

Uses: Use daylilies as ground cover and in flower borders. Everbloomers are good container plants.

Selections: Select a variety of cultivars with different bloom seasons. Rebloomers, including golden 'Stella De Oro', bloom best with rich soil and ample moisture.

Dianthus

Dianthus species
Perennials, Biennials, Annuals
Hardiness: Zones 3 to 10

Also called pinks, these popular flowers bloom in shades of pink, red, white, orange, purple, or cranberry. Blooms range from less than an inch to several inches wide. Plants range in height from just a few inches to several feet.

How to grow: Give plants full or nearly full sun and average to rich, well-drained soil. Refresh older plantings by dividing and resetting plants every few years. Named cultivars must be grown from cuttings or division, while others can be grown from seed. Germination requirements and times vary, so follow seed packet directions.

Uses: Grow pinks in beds, rock gardens, and containers.

Selections: Try different perennial species and Sweet William *(D. barbatus)*, a biennial. If you want fragrant blooms, like those of 'Firewitch', read descriptions or smell actual flowers: Not all are fragrant.

Echinacea

Echinacea purpurea
Perennial
Hardiness: Zones 3 to 10

Also called purple coneflower, this heat-tolerant native produces daisylike flowers with prickly, cone-shape centers and rose-purple, white, yellow, or orange petals (ray flowers) on stout stalks standing 2 to 4 feet high. Leaves are alternate, simple, and coarse.

How to grow: Coneflowers will grow in almost any well-drained garden soil in full sun. They are drought tolerant. Propagate by division in spring, or sow seeds in pots and set them outdoors. Plants self-sow, but seedlings will not necessarily resemble their parents.

Uses: Use coneflowers in beds and borders or in sunny wild-flower gardens. They make excellent cut flowers.

Selections: 'White Swan' has white flowers, and 'Magnus' produces huge rose-purple flowers. 'Paradiso Mix' includes vibrant colors in various shapes and sizes.

Four O'Clock

Mirabilis jalapa
Annual

The flowers of these old-fashioned annuals open in mid- to late afternoon and close the following morning. The bushy plants are 1 to 3 feet high and bear an abundance of fragrant, single-shade or marbled bicolor flowers in white, yellow, red, pink, or purple.

How to grow: Full sun or light shade and average to rich garden soil are ideal. The plants tolerate humidity, air pollution, heat, and drought. Sow seeds indoors, then move seedlings outdoors after danger of frost has passed. Seeds germinate in 7 to 10 days at 70°F. Four o'clocks form tubers that can be dug after frost in the fall and overwintered indoors for replanting in spring.

Uses: Plant four o'clocks along walks and near patios to enjoy their fragrant flowers.

Selections: Mixes such as 'High Tea' offer a range of vibrant colors.

Foxglove

Digitalis purpurea
Biennials, Perennials
Hardiness: Zones 4 to 9

Foxgloves produce gray-green leaves topped by 2- to 5-foot-tall, bloom-heavy stalks in early summer. The tubular, bell-shape flowers come in shades of pink, purple-pink, white, or creamy yellow, generally with a contrasting color speckling their throats.

How to grow: Give foxgloves light shade and average, moist, well-drained soil. Afternoon shade is important in hot climates. To grow foxgloves as biennials, sow seeds outdoors in pots in June or July, and transplant to the garden in fall. Cultivars like 'Foxy' will bloom the first year if sown indoors 8 to 10 weeks before the last frost date. Seeds germinate in 15 to 20 days at 70°F.

Uses: Plant foxgloves at the back of borders, against fences, near shrubs, or along woodlands.

Selections: Seed mixes such as 'Excelsior' offer a range of colors in each seed packet.

Gaillardia

Gaillardia × grandiflora
Annuals, Perennials
Hardiness: Zones 3 to 10

Gaillardias blossom over a long season in summer, showing off their yellow-and-red, 3- to 4-inch-wide, daisylike blooms with serrated petal tips. Also known as blanketflowers, these native North American wildflowers range in height from 10 inches to 3 feet.

How to grow: Full sun and any well-drained soil are all that both annual and perennial gaillardias require. The plants are drought tolerant. Sow annuals (actually tender perennials) indoors. Divide perennials regularly and propagate by division or cuttings. Deadhead them to keep them flowering.

Uses: Grow them in beds, borders, meadow plantings, and raised beds. Plant extras for cutting.

Selections: Flowers of both 'Goblin' and 'Arizona Sun' are red with yellow tips. Annual 'Sundance Bicolor' bears red-and-yellow pom-pom-shape blooms on 10- to 12-inch-tall plants.

Gazania

Gazania rigens
Annuals, Perennials
Hardiness: Zones 8 to 11

Grown for their brilliantly colored, daisylike flowers, gazanias are 8 to 12 inches tall and sport blooms in white, pink, bronze, red, yellow, or orange. Many selections feature petals with multiple contrasting colors.

How to grow: Plant gazanias in full sun and poor to average, well-drained soil. They tolerate drought, heat, and salt spray. Grow them as perennials from Zone 8 south. To grow as annuals, start seed indoors. Seeds germinate in 15 to 20 days at 70°F.

Uses: Plant gazanias in the front of beds and borders, and use them as ground cover in sunny, dry areas or in rock gardens.

Selections: 'Daybreak' series plants produce yellow petals striped with red. 'Daybreak Pink Shades' produce flowers in rich pink tones.

Geranium

Pelargonium species
Annual/Tender Perennial

Bushy tender perennials commonly grown as annuals, geraniums bear showy clusters of flowers in shades of red, pink, salmon, or white. Plants bloom from late spring to frost. Scented types have aromatic leaves but less-showy blooms.

How to grow: Give geraniums full sun and average to rich soil that's well drained. Deadhead to remove spent flowers. Start with plants or cuttings, or grow from seeds sown indoors 10 to 12 weeks before the last spring frost date. Seeds germinate in 7 to 10 days at 70° to 75°F. Bring plants indoors in fall for overwintering, or take and root cuttings to overwinter.

Uses: Use zonal geraniums in any sunny spot. All geraniums make excellent container plants.

Selections: In spring, garden centers stock a multitude of cultivars in a wide range of colors and bloom types.

Gerbera

Gerbera jamesonii
Annual/Tender Perennial
Hardiness: Zones 9 to 11

These tender perennials bear single to double daisylike flowers in shades of pink, orange, red, yellow, or white. Blooms are 4 inches or more in diameter, and plants range from 1 to 2 feet tall. They are hardy in Zones 9 to 11 and grown as annuals in cooler zones.

How to grow: Give gerberas rich, moist, well-drained soil and full sun, even though they tolerate partial shade. Buy plants, or sow seeds indoors 12 weeks before the last spring frost date. Seeds germinate in 10 to 14 days at 70° to 75°F. Transplant in spring after danger of frost has passed.

Uses: Mix gerberas with other low-growing flowers in beds or containers. Try digging and overwintering plants indoors, since established clumps bloom best.

Selections: 'California Giants' is a mix of colors with long stems for cutting.

Gomphrena

Gomphrena globosa
Annual

Also called globe amaranth, gomphrenas bear 1-inch-wide, papery-textured, cloverlike flowers all summer long; blooms come in violet, lavender, red, orange, pink, or creamy white. Plants are about 2 feet tall.

How to grow: Give gomphrenas full sun and any well-drained soil. Sow seeds indoors and move plants to the garden after the last frost date in spring, or sow outdoors after the last frost date. Keep the soil barely moist, never wet. Barely cover seeds with soil, because they need darkness to germinate, which takes 10 to 14 days at 65° to 75°F.

Uses: Mix gomphrenas with other flowers in beds and borders. Use dwarf types for edging. Grow extra plants for cutting and drying.

Selections: Dwarf 'Purple Buddy' is 9 to 12 inches tall. 'Strawberry Fields' is bright red. Several mixes are also available.

Hellebore

Helleborus × hybridus
Perennial
Hardiness: Zones 4 to 9

Also called Lenten roses, hellebores feature handsome evergreen leaves and late-winter to very early-spring flowers in shades of cream, burgundy, pink, or purple. Flowers are nodding, saucer-shape, and either single or double.

How to grow: Plant hellebores in partial shade and average to rich, well-drained soil. Start with plants, or sow seeds in pots outdoors. Cut back leaves in midwinter so flowers show to best effect.

Uses: Hellebores are ideal for shady beds and borders. They also make an excellent ground cover. But keep in mind: All parts of this plant are poisonous.

Selections: The best hybrids available in America today are clones. 'Kingston Cardinal' and 'Onyx Odyssey' are great double varieties but are available only as transplants.

Hibiscus

Hibiscus moscheutos
Perennial
Hardiness: Zones 5 to 10

Also called rose mallow, this native American wildflower bears flowers up to 10 inches across in shades of pink, red, or white. The shrub-size plants bloom for much of the summer and form tough clumps that can reach 8 feet in height.

How to grow: Give plants full sun to light shade and moist, average to rich soil. Buy plants, or start from seed. Growth emerges late in spring, so it's wise to mark the locations of clumps.

Uses: Use mallows in wild gardens, in areas with damp soil, or toward the back of a bed or border.

Selections: Numerous hybrids are suitable for adding a tropical flair to gardens. 'Southern Belle' produces huge flowers in red, rose, pink, and white and grows to 4 feet tall. 'Lord Baltimore' bears red flowers and reaches 8 feet in height.

Hollyhock

Alcea rosea
Biennials, Perennials
Hardiness: Zones 3 to 9

Old-fashioned garden favorites, hollyhocks have upright stalks covered with showy, single or double flowers. Blooms come in shades of pink, white, red, maroon, or yellow. Each flower is 2 to 4 inches wide. Full-size plants reach 4 to 6 feet tall; dwarf types range from 2 to 3 feet.

How to grow: Plant in full sun and average, well-drained soil. Stake tall selections on windy sites. Replace plants every other year to minimize diseases such as rust. Plants self-sow, but seedlings may not resemble their parents. Sow seeds indoors or outside in individual pots to minimize transplant stress. Germination takes 10 to 24 days at 70°F.

Uses: Plant standard hollyhocks along fences or buildings or toward the rear of flower gardens.

Selections: 'Country Romance' produces single-flower blooms in a range of colors.

Hosta

Hosta species
Perennial
Hardiness: Zones 3 to 9

Hostas produce clumps of handsome leaves that may be green or variously marked with white, cream, or blue-green. Clumps are topped by stalks of white or purple flowers in summer. Plants range from tiny clumps only inches tall to large 2- to 3-foot-tall perennials for use anywhere in the shade.

How to grow: Plant hostas in partial to full shade with average to rich, well-drained soil. They tolerate more sun in the North and need more shade in hot climates. Start with plants or divisions of selections grown for their showy leaves.

Uses: Hostas are the backbone of the shade garden. Use smaller types as edging and large ones in beds, as specimens, or as ground covers.

Selections: Hundreds of cultivars that sport handsome leaves are available. Plant several sizes and leaf patterns.

Impatiens

Impatiens hybrids
Annual

Glorious shade-garden plants, impatiens are mounding, 12- to 15-inch-tall annuals that are covered with flowers from summer to frost. Single or double flowers come in white, pink, rose, orange, scarlet, burgundy, or lavender.

How to grow: Give impatiens partial shade to shade and average, well-drained soil. Bloom diminishes in deep shade. Start with plants, or sow seeds indoors 10 to 12 weeks before the last spring frost date. Germination takes 10 to 20 days at 75°F.

Uses: Grow impatiens as edging, as ground cover, or in colorful drifts added to shady beds and borders. Dwarf types are especially effective in containers.

Selections: There are many mixes that offer a variety of colors. African hybrids have orchidlike blooms; New Guinea impatiens bear large flowers, 2 to 3 inches across.

Lavender

Lavandula angustifolia
Perennial
Hardiness: Zones 5 to 10

Richly fragrant lavender is an aromatic herb that bears terminal clusters of lavender, dark purple, pink, or white flowers in summer. The gray-green, evergreen leaves are as fragrant as the flowers. Plants are 2 to 3 feet tall and shrubby.

How to grow: Give plants full sun and well-drained, average to sandy soil. Plants are quite drought tolerant once established and also tolerate light shade. In the spring, prune back the deadwood, and shape the plants. Start with plants, or sow seeds outdoors in pots.

Uses: Grow plants in beds and borders, as low hedges, in herb gardens, or in rock gardens.

Selections: 'Lady' is an award winner that flowers the first year from seeds. 'Hidcote' is compact, growing 1½ to 2 feet tall.

Lisianthus

Eustoma grandiflorum
Annual

Also called prairie gentian, this plant is native from the Midwest to Mexico and bears somewhat poppylike, cup-shape flowers in bluish-purple, blue, pink, or white. Plants grow up to 3 feet tall. Although most are single-flowered, semidouble and double-flowered selections are available.

How to grow: Give lisianthus full sun and rich, moist soil. To grow them as annuals, sow seeds 3 months before the last spring frost date. Use individual pots, since they have taproots and are difficult to transplant. Germination takes 10 to 20 days at 75° to 80°F. Pinch out the growing tips to induce branching and greater flowering.

Uses: Grow lisianthus in cutting gardens, beds, and containers.

Selections: Many mixes are available. Single-color offerings are great as cut flowers and for landscape effect.

Marigold

Tagetes species
Annual

All-American marigolds are a garden mainstay. Plants range from 8 inches to 3 feet in height and bear single to fully double flowers in yellow, gold, orange, or creamy white. French marigolds are bushier and more compact than American types, which have larger flowers.

How to grow: Plant marigolds in full sun and average to rich, moist, well-drained soil. They tolerate dry conditions. Start with plants, or sow seeds indoors. Seeds germinate in 5 to 7 days at 65° to 75°F. Move transplants to the garden as soon as all danger of frost has passed.

Uses: Grow taller types toward the center or rear of beds and borders. Use French marigolds as edging and in containers.

Selections: Hundreds of color and form variations are available. Plant a mix or a single color, depending on your garden design.

Monarda

Monarda didyma
Perennial
Hardiness: Zones 3 to 7

These hardy native American plants are also known as bee balm and bergamot. Plants feature aromatic leaves and stems that are sturdy, square, and 2 to 4 feet tall. They are topped with shaggy-looking clusters of flowers in bright red, pink, purple, or white from mid- to late summer.

How to grow: Full sun and slightly moist soil are best for monardas; they become somewhat floppy in shade. To reduce mildew problems, plant where air circulation is good. These plants are vigorous spreaders: Dig and divide the clumps every few years to keep them in bounds. Propagate by division or seed sown outdoors.

Uses: Both hummingbirds and butterflies adore monardas. Use them in borders and wild gardens.

Selections: 'Jacob Cline' is extremely mildew resistant. 'Petite Delight' is 12 to 15 inches tall and bears pink flowers.

Morning Glory

Ipomoea
Annual

These easy-to-grow, dependable vines bear trumpet-shape blooms in true blue, purple, pink, crimson red, or white, with many bicolor combinations available. Blooms open from dawn to midmorning, each lasting only a day. Plants have heart-shaped leaves and reach 10 feet in height/length.

How to grow: Give morning glories full sun and average soil. Soak seeds in water a day before planting. Sow outdoors when all danger of frost has passed or indoors 4 to 6 weeks before the last spring frost. Germination takes a week at 70°F. Plants need a trellis or other support to climb on.

Uses: Plant along fences, trellises, or shrubs that they can climb.

Selections: 'Heavenly Blue' is a rich blue heirloom. 'Scarlett O'Hara' bears crimson red flowers. Related convolvulus *(Convolvulus tricolor)* produces bushy, 14-inch plants with pink, blue, purple, or rose morning-glory-type flowers.

Nasturtium

Tropaeolum majus
Annual

Nasturtiums bear nearly round leaves and yellow, red, maroon, or orange flowers. Flowers and foliage are edible and peppery tasting. Plants are either vinelike and 4 to 10 feet in length or about 12 inches tall and bushy.

How to grow: Give nasturtiums full sun and dry, sandy, well-drained soil. Cool, dry summers suit them best. Sow seeds outdoors after last spring frost, or start them in individual pots indoors 4 to 5 weeks before the last frost date. Tie vining types to supports; they have no means of attachment. Germination takes 10 to 14 days at 65° to 70°F.

Uses: Bushy types are good for borders, beds, and edging. Tie vining types to fences or trellises. Use either in containers.

Selections: Many mixes are available, including 'Dwarf Double Jewel', 'Double Gleam', and 'Alaska'.

Nicotiana

Nicotiana alata
Annual

Also known as flowering tobacco, nicotianas come in white, pink, maroon, lavender, chartreuse, red, or yellow. Flowers are trumpet-shape with starry faces. The plants grow 2 to 3 feet tall. Some nicotianas are fragrant.

How to grow: Plant in full sun or partial shade in rich, moist, well-drained soil. Afternoon shade is best in hot climates. Buy plants, or start from seed. Sow indoors and move to the garden after the last spring frost date, or sow outdoors after the last frost. Seeds germinate in 10 to 15 days at 70° to 75°F.

Uses: Grow nicotianas in containers or in flower beds with other annuals.

Selections: Select carefully if you want fragrant flowers. 'Heaven Scent' is fragrant and comes in a mix of colors. Related *Nicotiana sylvestris* is a very fragrant, 4-foot-tall species with white flowers.

Pansy

Viola × wittrockiana
Annual

Low-growing, cool-season annuals, pansies produce flowers that are 2 to 5 inches across and come in a complete range of colors. Solid-color selections are available, but many feature facelike markings in bright contrasting colors.

How to grow: Give pansies full sun—partial shade in hot climates—and rich, moist soil. From Zone 7 south, plant them in fall for winter to spring bloom. Elsewhere, plant in early spring as soon as the ground thaws. Shear leggy plants back halfway to force new growth and bloom. Buy plants, or start from seeds sown 6 to 8 weeks prior to planting outdoors. Seeds germinate in 10 to 15 days at 68°F.

Uses: Plant pansies anywhere you want spots of color.

Selections: Many mixes and colors are available. 'Atlas Mix', with 3-inch flowers in a wide range of colors, is especially cold hardy.

Phlox

Phlox species
Annuals, Perennials
Hardiness: Zones 3 to 9

Perennial phlox range from spring-blooming, 2-inch-high moss phlox *(P. subulata)* to 3- to 4-foot-tall garden phlox *(P. paniculata)*, which bears showy clusters of fragrant flowers in summer. Blooms come in white, rose, pink, purple, lavender, blue, or magenta.

How to grow: Provide rich, moist, well-drained soil in full sun or light shade. Garden phlox is susceptible to powdery mildew, so buy disease-resistant cultivars and thin out stems in spring to improve air circulation. Divide clumps every 3 years to keep them vigorous. Propagate by division, or sow seeds. Sow annual phlox *(P. drummondii)* outdoors after last spring frost date, or start indoors 4 to 6 weeks earlier.

Uses: Grow garden phlox in borders. Low-growing species can be used in beds or as ground cover.

Selections: 'David' bears white flowers and is extremely mildew resistant.

Petunia

Petunia × hybrida
Annual

Petunias come in different sizes and forms, but all bear showy, trumpet-shape flowers in shades of pink, lavender, purple, or red. Many bicolors are available, too. Blooms may be single or double and range from about 2 to 4 inches wide.

How to grow: Full sun to light shade and average to rich, well-drained soil suit petunias best, although they tolerate poor soil. Deadhead regularly, and shear plants back halfway in midsummer to promote branching and more flowers. Start with plants, or sow seeds indoors 10 to 12 weeks before the last spring frost date. Seeds germinate in 10 to 12 days at 70° to 75°F.

Uses: Beds, borders, walkways, paths, and containers can all accommodate an abundance of petunias.

Selections: Wave Series hybrids, including 'Purple Wave', all bear abundant small flowers on 3- to 5-foot-wide spreading plants.

Poppy

Papaver and *Eschscholzia* species
Annuals, Perennials
Hardiness: Zones 3 to 8

Gardeners grow poppies for their silky, crinkly petaled, early summer flowers. Oriental poppy *(P. orientale)* is a 2- to 4-foot-tall perennial with showy 4- to 6-inch-wide flowers. California poppy *(E. californica)* bears 3-inch blooms on foot-tall plants in summer. For both, flowers come in a range of colors, including orange, pink, red, salmon, and white. California poppies also come in yellow.

How to grow: Give poppies full sun and average, well-drained soil. Deadhead to reduce self-sowing. Sow California poppies outdoors in early spring; plant in fall in mild climates. Seeds germinate in 10 days at 60°F. Start perennials from plants or seeds sown outdoors in pots.

Uses: Plant poppies among other flowers in beds or borders.

Selections: Improved Oriental poppies such as 'Allegro' and 'Pizzicato Mix' are stunning.

Portulaca

Portulaca grandiflora
Annual

Also called moss rose and rose moss, this nearly prostrate annual bears an abundance of small flowers in jewellike colors, including yellow, gold, orange, crimson, pink, lavender, purple, and white. Blooms may be single or double and open in sunny weather.

How to grow: Portulacas need full sun and light, sandy, well-drained soil. They tolerate heat and drought but bloom better with adequate moisture. Sow seeds outdoors after the last spring frost date, or start indoors 4 to 6 weeks earlier. Either way, wait until the soil has warmed up to move plants or sow seed outdoors. Seeds germinate in 10 to 15 days at 70° to 80°F.

Uses: Grow portulaca as a ground cover or as edging on problem spots.

Selections: 'Sundial Hybrid' is a mix with blooms that remain open longer than other portulacas.

Rudbeckia

Rudbeckia species
Biennials, Perennials
Hardiness: Zones 3 to 9

Rudbeckias bear daisylike flowers with dark centers and gold, yellow, orange, rust, or maroon petals, many with bands of contrasting colors. Black-eyed Susan *(R. hirta)* blooms the first year from seed and is often grown as an annual. Orange coneflower *(R. fulgida)* is a 2- to 3-foot-tall perennial.

How to grow: Give rudbeckias full sun and poor to average soil. They tolerate drought. Start with plants, or sow seeds indoors 8 to 10 weeks before the last spring frost date. Transplant to the garden after the last spring frost date. Seeds germinate in 5 to 10 days at 70° to 75°F. Deadhead to encourage new flowers.

Uses: Grow rudbeckias in any sunny spot.

Selections: Biennial 'Indian Summer' bears 6- to 9-inch-wide golden flowers. Perennial 'Goldsturm' bears 3- to 4-inch-wide flowers.

Salvia

***Salvia* species**
Annuals, Perennials
Hardiness: Zones 4 to 9

Grown for their showy spikes of small, two-lipped flowers, salvias come in red, pink, violet, lavender, blue, or white. Many feature fragrant foliage. Plants range from 1 foot to 4 or more feet tall, depending on the species. Hardiness varies, and many annual salvias are tender perennials that are hardy from Zone 7 or 8 south. Overwinter these plants indoors in cold climates.

How to grow: Give plants full sun or partial shade and average, moist soil. Start with plants, or sow seeds indoors and move transplants to the garden after the danger of frost has passed. Seeds germinate in 12 to 15 days at 70° to 75°F.

Uses: Grow salvias in beds and borders.

Selections: 'Lady in Red' is an award-winning annual. 'Victoria' is a classic blue annual. 'Rose Queen' bears spikes of pink flowers.

Scabiosa

***Scabiosa* species**
Annuals, Perennials
Hardiness: Zones 3 to 8

Also called pincushion flower, scabiosas bear ruffled, buttonlike blooms in pink, violet, maroon, blue, or white. Plants are 1 foot to 2½ feet tall.

How to grow: Give plants full sun and average to rich, well-drained soil. Overly moist soil causes root rot. Sow seeds outdoors after the last spring frost date, or sow indoors 4 to 6 weeks before that date and move plants to the garden after danger of frost has passed. Seeds germinate in 10 to 15 days at 70° to 75°F. Deadhead to prolong bloom.

Uses: Grow in mixed beds and borders or in cottage gardens.

Selections: Mixes of annual sweet scabious *(S. atropurpurea)*, including 'Summer Berries', are available. 'Butterfly Blue' is an outstanding, long-blooming perennial scabiosa *(S. columbaria)*. Starflower *(S. stellata)* makes a good dried flower.

Snapdragon

Antirrhinum majus
Annual

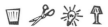

Best known for their two-lipped flowers that children love to snap open, snapdragons now come in double and open-face forms that no longer snap. Plants bear stalks of flowers in white, cream, yellow, burgundy, red, pink, orange, or bronze. Heights vary from 10 inches to 4 feet.

How to grow: Give plants full sun and rich, moist, well-drained soil. Sow seeds indoors, and transplant after the last spring frost date. Pinch young plants to encourage branching. Tall varieties need staking. Deadhead to encourage repeat bloom.

Uses: Use the tall selections for the back of the border and as cut flowers. Dwarf types are great as edging and in containers.

Selections: Many sizes and flower types are available in a range of colors. Select the height that suits your garden.

Sunflower

Helianthus annuus
Annual

These North American natives can be 15-foot-high giants or foot-tall dwarfs in containers. All bear showy daisy-type flowers with a broad central eye and yellow, gold, maroon, or creamy yellow petals. Many petals are bicolored, and flowers can be single or double.

How to grow: Grow sunflowers in full sun and average, moist but well-drained soil. Plants tolerate heat and drought. Sow seeds outdoors after the last spring frost date, or sow indoors for an early start. Seeds germinate in 10 to 15 days at 70° to 75°F.

Uses: Use dwarf types in beds and borders and taller selections at the back of borders or as a natural screen.

Selections: Choose cultivars by height and flower size to suit your garden site and needs. Plant seed-types like 'Mammoth Russian' for the edible seeds.

Sweet Pea

Lathyrus odoratus
Annual

Sweet peas are vining plants that vigorously climb fences or other supports to a height of 6 or 8 feet. The flowers can be pink, white, red, lavender, or purple.

How to grow: Give sweet peas full sun and rich, moist, well-drained soil. They require cool weather. In areas with mild winters, grow them fall through winter. Elsewhere, sow seeds outdoors as soon as the soil has thawed and can be worked, or sow indoors in individual pots 4 to 6 weeks before that and transplant outside as early as possible. Pinch seedlings to encourage branching, and mulch plants to keep the soil cool. Seeds germinate in 10 to 14 days at 55° to 65°F.

Uses: Train sweet peas up and across fences and trellises.

Selections: For scented flowers, choose selections described as fragrant, including 'High Scent' and 'Eckford's Finest Mix'.

Torenia

Torenia fournieri
Annual

Torenias are wonderful for shade in hot, humid climates. Plants are 8 to 12 inches tall, with flowers that resemble open-face snapdragons. Flowers come in purple-blue, violet, pink, or maroon. The flowers have "faces" in contrasting colors, somewhat like pansies.

How to grow: Give plants partial shade and rich, moist, well-drained soil. In frost-free areas, grow them for winter and spring display. They like high humidity and won't tolerate drying out. Sow seeds indoors 10 to 12 weeks before planting outdoors, and move transplants or purchased plants outdoors after all danger of frost has passed. Germination takes 10 to 15 days at 70°F.

Uses: Combine torenias with other shade-lovers such as begonias and coleus.

Selections: 'Clown Mix' and 'Happy Faces' both bear blooms in a mix of purple-blues, pinks, maroon-reds, and white.

Verbena

Verbena × hybrida
Annual

Trailing or mounding plants, verbenas range from 8 inches to 1½ feet tall. They are grown for their showy, rounded clusters of tiny trumpet-shape flowers. Blooms come in violet, purple, rose, red, salmon-orange, or white.

How to grow: Give plants full sun and average or sandy, well-drained soil. Start from plants, or sow seeds indoors 12 to 14 weeks before the last spring frost date, and move plants to the garden after danger of frost has passed. Barely cover the seeds with soil, as darkness is necessary for germination. Germination takes 2 to 3 weeks at 65° to 75°F.

Uses: Use trailing types over walls and in rock gardens. Mounding cultivars are good for beds and borders.

Selections: Many cultivars are available. 'Showtime' and 'Spring-time' are good mixes. 'Peaches N Cream' is soft salmon-orange.

Vinca

Catharanthus roseus
Annual

Also called Madagascar periwinkle, this heat-loving annual bears round, 5-petaled flowers in white, pink, pinkish red, lavender, or purple. Many blooms have a contrasting white eye.

How to grow: Give plants full sun and average to rich, well-drained soil. Plants thrive in heat and humidity. They are perennials in Zone 10. Start with plants, or sow seeds indoors 3 to 4 months before the last spring frost date. Move to garden after all danger of frost has passed. Germination takes 14 to 21 days at 70° to 75°F. Cover seed, since darkness aids germination. Take root cuttings to overwinter plants, if desired.

Uses: Use vincas as edging or ground cover, or plant drifts of them in flower beds.

Selections: A number of mixes are available, including 'Magic Carpet Mix'. Award-winning 'First Kiss Blueberry' bears blue-purple blooms.

Viola

Viola species
Annual

Cousins of modern-day pansies, violas bear charming pansylike flowers from spring to midsummer. Blooms come in a wide range of colors, including yellow, pink, purple, lavender, and white. Most are marked with contrasting colors, and plants range from 6 to 10 inches tall.

How to grow: Grow violas in full sun to part shade and rich, moist soil. From Zone 7 south, plant violas in the fall for winter to spring bloom. Start with plants, or sow seeds indoors, then move them to the garden a few weeks before the last spring frost date. Seeds germinate in 10 to 15 days at 68°F.

Uses: Add violas to beds, borders, and containers.

Selections: Old-fashioned Johnny Jump-Up with yellow, purple, and lavender blooms is just one of many brightly colored violas.

Zinnia

Zinnia species
Annual

Beloved garden flowers, zinnias come in a wide range of colors, sizes, and flower forms. Flowers may be single, semidouble, or double and range in width from 2 to 5 inches. Flowers come in red, yellow, pink, magenta, orange, white, or green. Heights vary from 6 inches to 4 feet.

How to grow: Give zinnias full sun and rich, well-drained soil. Powdery mildew can be a problem in humid weather. Sow seeds outdoors after the last spring frost date. Sow seeds indoors 4 weeks before that date for earlier bloom. Seeds germinate in 5 to 7 days at 70° to 75°F. Deadhead to prolong bloom.

Uses: Plant dwarf types as edging. Use taller zinnias with other annuals or in masses in beds and borders.

Selections: Many colors and mixes are available. Profusion and Zahara series are disease-resistant plants.

USDA Plant Hardiness Zone Map

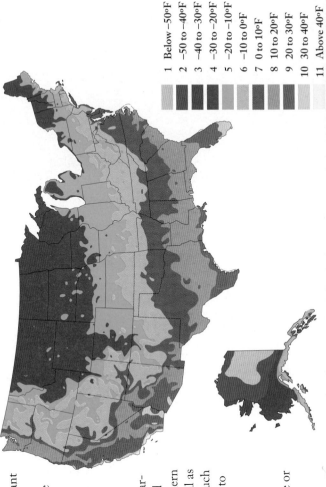

1	Below –50°F
2	–50 to –40°F
3	–40 to –30°F
4	–30 to –20°F
5	–20 to –10°F
6	–10 to 0°F
7	0 to 10°F
8	10 to 20°F
9	20 to 30°F
10	30 to 40°F
11	Above 40°F

The U.S. Department of Agriculture Plant Hardiness Zone Map divides North America into 11 zones based on average minimum winter temperatures, with Zone 1 being the coldest and Zone 11 the warmest. (Hawaii is in Zone 11.)

This map should only be used as a general guideline, since the lines of separation between zones are not as clear-cut as they appear. Plants recommended for one zone might do well in the southern part of the adjoining colder zone, as well as in neighboring warmer zones. Factors such as altitude, exposure to wind, proximity to a large body of water, and amount of available sunlight also contribute to a plant's winter hardiness. Because snow cover insulates plants, winters with little or no snow tend to be more damaging to marginally hardy varieties.